SOLDIER OF CHANGE

SOLDIER OF CHANGE

*From the Closet to the Forefront
of the Gay Rights Movement*

STEPHEN SNYDER-HILL

Foreword by GEORGE TAKEI

Potomac Books
An imprint of the University of Nebraska Press

Library of Congress
Cataloging-in-Publication Data
Snyder-Hill, Stephen.
Soldier of change: from the closet
to the forefront of the gay rights
movement / Stephen Snyder-
Hill; foreword by George Takei.
pages   cm
ISBN 978-1-61234-697-7
(cloth: alk. paper)
1. Gay military personnel—
United States. 2. United States.
Army—Officers—Biography.
3. Gay men—United States—
Biography. 4. Gay activists—United
States—Biography. 5. Columbus
(Ohio)—Biography. I. Title. II. Title:
From the closet to the forefront
of the gay rights movement.
UB418.G38S69 2014
355.0092—dc23   [B]
2014004308

Set in Lyon Text by Renni Johnson.
Designed by N. Putens.

To the love of my life, Joshua. You are the fuel to my fire, and you bring out the best in me. I never think of me, I think of us. We are one and will always be. I love you with all of my life. I told you that if you waited for me when I went to war, you would be the one . . . you are the one.

Contents

Foreword

I first heard about Steve Hill (now Snyder-Hill, after he married his longtime partner, Joshua) the way most of the world did—on the news. For a Republican presidential primary debate in September of 2011, a gay soldier serving in Iraq had submitted a videotaped question in which he both came out on national television and confronted a scenario that had been on many of our minds. Captain Hill explained that he had been required to lie about who he was when he joined the army, and then he poignantly asked the candidates this: "As part of your presidency, do you intend to circumvent the progress that has been made for gay and lesbian soldiers in the military?" In other words, would they, if elected, continue to permit gays and lesbians to serve openly and honorably, or would they return our military to the shame of the "Don't Ask, Don't Tell" policy that had been recently abolished by President Obama?

It was a fair question, posed by someone who risked his life every day in the service of his country. Like so many others, however, Captain Hill's legal status was in limbo. Would he have to leave military service, having relied upon President Obama's abolition of the policy only to see it reinstated by a new commander-in-chief? Or if he stayed, would he face renewed ridicule, prejudice, and job discrimination?

For merely asking this question, Captain Hill was met by scattered boos from the crowd, boos that grew into a chorus. It was appalling and outrageous. Apparently, the mere acknowledgment by a soldier that he was gay was enough to rile the crowd. Far-right conservatives don't appreciate much of anything that disrupts their own worldview, and strapping young soldiers who up-end gay stereotypes tend to do that. (Jon Stewart, remarking on Captain Hill, observed that if he turned into the Hulk, his arms would stay the same size. They would just turn green.)

Or was the booing because Captain Hill actually had posed a legitimate question—one that put conservatives squarely on the spot? Gay equality is no doubt a "wedge" issue, one that used to be trotted out to galvanize conservatives and win elections for the right. But with public perception changing, the issue is now one increasingly posed by the *left* to call out bigotry and hypocrisy—the very kind conservatives demonstrate when they rail over keeping the government out of their gun closets while inviting it straight into our bedrooms.

Conservatives also don't like these types of questions because they know they are on the losing side in the Culture Wars and, by extension, history. Recent polls show that as many as 70 percent of young people support marriage equality, and even higher percentages support job nondiscrimination for LGBTs. But still the far-right, apparently represented by the kind of folks who attend Republican primary debates, clings steadfastly to the past, hoping that by some miracle the gays will simply go away or, if they won't, will keep their mouths shut.

The audience reaction reflected both of these impulses. The boos underscored for me the urgent need for the military to stand firm and support its members, regardless of sexual orientation. Being gay, at least by most accounts, is an immutable, innate characteristic, as much a part of one's identity as skin color or ethnic origin. It has nothing to do with job performance, and it only can be said to disrupt "unit cohesion" in the armed forces where prejudice and animus is permitted to take root and spread. It is the job of the army command to ensure that unit cohesion is maintained at a high level, not at the lowest common denominator of intolerance.

When I watched the clip played and replayed on television, I was livid. I took to social media to speak out against what had occurred, tweeting to my fans my anger:

> Audience at Rep. debate boos gay soldier Stephen Hill, now serving in Iraq, for saying "I had to lie about who I was." #HaveTheyNoDecency?

I deliberately chose that hashtag because the witch hunts for gays in the military, which had only recently ended by presidential decree, reminded me of the terrifying days of McCarthyism, where the weight of the government was put behind ferreting out suspected communists. It was clear that our hard-fought victories for equality would have to be shored up, and that we would have to remain vigilant against an inevitable backlash by the right. Decency would have to prevail.

From my own base, the response was overwhelmingly positive toward Captain Hill and condemning not only of the audience members who booed him but of the candidates who stood by and said nothing. Indeed, the only thing more shameful than the disrespect shown to Captain Hill by the audience was the total indifference and silence of the Republican presidential candidates. Not one of them admonished the crowd for its behavior. Not one of them spoke out in defense of a bona fide hero. Even the more socially liberal Republican candidates standing on that stage remained disgracefully silent, too cowed by the zealots in their midst to say and do the right thing. Had they, as I'd suggested, no decency by which to guide their consciences, or were they simply afraid that they would lose support among conservative voters—the ones who typically decide primary races?

True leadership is not just about knowing what the right thing is; it is doing the right thing even when you know it might be unpopular. It was this indifference that had me most disappointed. As Dr. Martin Luther King once so aptly said, "In the end, we will remember not the words of our enemies but the silence of our friends."

No matter what the candidates' *personal* views on homosexuality were, or whether they believed gays and lesbians should be allowed to serve openly in the military, there were two other values that went wholly ignored in that telling moment.

First, the president and commander-in-chief of the U.S. military, in consultation with his leading military advisors, already had lifted "Don't Ask, Don't Tell." It was both executive and military official policy that gays and lesbians would no longer have to hide who they were. Captain Hill was doing just that, and he had every right under law to self-identify publicly as gay without repercussion to his career. The boos and the deafening silence that followed were a slap in the face to the rule of law.

Second, Captain Hill had served in Iraq and was as deserving of respect and gratitude as any of our soldiers and veterans. The supposed leaders of the GOP, a party that typically prides itself on "supporting our troops" at all cost even when one disagrees with the mission, had again demonstrated their hypocrisy. (To his credit, when asked about this incident, former presidential candidate John McCain, who had fought to maintain "Don't Ask, Don't Tell," stated that we "should honor every man and woman who is serving in the military." While not an outright condemnation, at least it was still something of a rebuke to the disgraceful and some might say even childish behavior exhibited.)

Senator Rick Santorum of Pennsylvania provided the sole response to Captain Hill's question. He cynically played to the bigots in the room by raising what I call the "ick" factor, bombastically proclaiming that gay sex has no place in the military. Captain Hill of course had not asked about sex. He had asked about identity and the right to live and serve openly. It's rather interesting to me how preoccupied Senator Santorum appears to be about gay sex for someone who supposedly cannot stand the thought of it. Senator Santorum then added that the military is "no place for social experimentation" and that he would return our gay and lesbian soldiers to the closet where, plainly, he believed they belonged.

Senator Santorum's attitude was fodder for those who want to further stigmatize and even physically harm our LGBT soldiers. The notion that they must hide their identity carries with it an unspoken position that gays and lesbians, when serving openly, will leer at and prey upon their fellow servicemembers. Again and again, the rights of soldiers not to have to shower, undress, and share close quarters with someone who is gay are cited as justification for keeping LGBT soldiers deep in the closet. But this reasoning elevates prejudice as a basis for further prejudice. It is a vicious and unending cycle that only determined leadership and courage can break.

This specious logic also completely ignores the fact that gays and lesbians shower and change with heterosexuals in locker rooms in private gyms every day across the country, and they commonly share rooms in boarding schools and universities with their straight classmates without incident. The concern for the privacy of our soldiers grants them less credit to deal with the presence of a gay person than even the average civilian and is therefore no less than insulting to our troops. It also presumptuously assumes that every gay person will be attracted to a straight colleague, which is most assuredly not the case. Sorry, Senator Santorum. I really wouldn't want to see you naked.

But on a more serious note, Senator Santorum's response was as ignorant of history as it was baldly bigoted. To claim that the military is no place to advance "social experimentation" or to set aspirational social goals for the nation as a whole overlooks the history of racial desegregation within the military's ranks. Indeed, as early as 1948, President Truman, in Executive Order

9981, ordered the rank and file of the military to be racially desegregated, long before the civil rights movement forced the same of our schools and other institutions. To be sure, racial integration of our armed forces occurred over the howls and protests of certain top commanders and conservative lawmakers, people of the same ilk who would rather gays and lesbians weren't given a place at all in our military today.

It is quite revealing, in fact, to look back to that time and review the arguments against racial desegregation of our armed forces. The military working group assigned to study proposed racial integration of the navy in the 1940s drew conclusions about interracial mixing that sound remarkably similar to recent concerns over gay men in proximity with their straight counterparts:

> Men on board ship live in particularly close association; in their messes, one man sits beside another; their hammocks or bunks are close together; in their common tasks they work side by side; and in particular tasks such as those of a gun's crew, they form a closely knit, highly coordinated team. How many white men would choose, of their own accord, that their closest associates in sleeping quarters, at mess, and in a gun's crew should be of another race?

These concerns sound preposterous today, particularly after we have had not only an African American chairman of the Joint Chiefs of Staff in Colin Powell but also an African American commander-in-chief in Barack Obama.

It was the familiar "ick" factor that underlay the fear and trepidation against racial mixing back in the 1940s, the same visceral reaction many today have toward gays and lesbians. People imagine gays—and gay men in particular—to be sexual deviants and predators. Many continue to be taught in their churches, conditioned by their peers in school, or led by the media and pop culture to be repulsed by the notion of gay physical affection. Gay love is to many, even still today, as unfamiliar as interracial love or even interracial friendship was to society in the 1940s. It is fair to say most of America at that time was repulsed by the idea of racial mixing, so much so that blacks would not be expected to use the same water fountains or bathrooms as whites or be in the same sleeping quarters or mess hall. Growing up in California, as an Asian American I would not have been permitted to marry a white at the time. Now I'm married to a white dude—how things change over time.

And so they did in the military, too. Contrary to the dire predictions of the anti-integrationists, the army did not crumble, soldiers obeyed the command of their leaders as they are expected to do, and race became, over time, increasingly a nonissue in the military.

It is soldiers like Stephen Snyder-Hill, who last year was promoted to major in the U.S. Army, who will effect that change with respect to LGBT soldiers, simply by continuing to represent the values that the military ought to stand for—honor, courage, and valor. I salute Major Snyder-Hill for demonstrating all three in his history-making question and, as this book poignantly reveals, in his continuing battle for equality for LGBT persons everywhere. He truly is a "Soldier of Change."

George Takei

Preface

First I need to cover my bases. My opinions, beliefs, and statements are mine only. They do not reflect the beliefs of the Department of Defense or the United States Army. The army JAG lawyers told me I always needed to cover that. Check.

Now for my own disclaimer. I talk about certain events that I have personally witnessed or experienced, but this does not mean all soldiers can be judged based on my experiences. There are a lot of great people and some not-so-great people in the armed forces. This book is not designed in any way to make the army or soldiers look bad; it is a story of my personal experience under "Don't Ask, Don't Tell." Soldiers sacrifice a lot to serve their country. LGBT soldiers sacrificed so much more before the end of DADT. Soldiers have also gotten kudos, but not us. Now it is our turn to tell our stories.

Acknowledgments

I dedicated a lot of thought to all the people I want to acknowledge in this book, but first and foremost, it all comes back to this: I owe everything to all of my LGBT brothers and sisters who have answered the call to serve their country. We are a part of history, more than ever before, now that we are allowed to tell our stories.

People will never understand the sacrifices soldiers make to serve their country, all the way up to and sometimes including their lives. But until September 20, 2011, we gave so much more. This book is for every unnamed soldier who had to lie about who he or she spent the weekend with and for everyone who had to make up stories to serve the country they love. This is for people like my friend Lee, who was kicked out and humiliated during "Don't Ask, Don't Tell" but was the first person in line to serve his country again right after the policy was repealed. There are thousands of stories like his. This book is never about me; it is about us.

Next is my best friend, my life partner, my love, my husband, Joshua. You will never know what you mean to me and what you have done for me. Without you I don't know if I would have the strength to fight so strongly for what I believe in. Though you have never been in the military, you are a soldier. You are the fuel to my fire, my conviction, and my motivation. I do not possess the skills to articulate in words what you mean to me. On May 3, 2011, my life was changed.

There are many things in my life that have seemed like a million stars lined up perfectly so things could work out just the way they did. It had to have been fate that I met Meredith Camel, my editor, on my honeymoon cruise. From the moment we met, we created a bond that carried us through the creation of this book. Without her I would not have been able to tell this story. No editor in the world could have put as much heart into making sure this was done right!

I also want to acknowledge my parents. I am what I am because of what they taught me. They never turned their backs on me through tough times and coming out. They loved me and encouraged me all the way, gay or not. They were the ones who taught me to stand up and fight for my rights. They are the people I want to be.

I also would not be who I am without my brother and his family. Growing up, we were best friends, and people always say we are exactly alike. I have never told him, but that makes me very proud. I have always been proud of him, and he was the catalyst for me to want to start living my life as a truth.

The truth is, everyone in my life has influenced me to become who I am. If I wrote about you in this book, then you understand the significance of the part you played in my quest for equality and my activism, and I thank you. And to all the heroes in my life I never had the privilege of knowing—Harvey Milk, Leonard Matlovich, Rosa Parks, Martin Luther King Jr., and many more—what you all achieved, and what some of you died for, will go on to influence and inspire generations for years to come.

Last but never least, as corny as it may be, I have to acknowledge my babies, Macho, Gizmo, Hummer, and Spanky. I always felt so bad leaving for deployment and not being able to explain to them why I was about to vanish out of their lives for a year. These pets have gotten me through some very tough times with unconditional love . . . if only humans could do the same.

SOLDIER OF CHANGE

1 A Leap of Faith

We boarded the plane. I sat down and closed my eyes. I looked down at my watch, December 4, 2010, 22:16. Could this be happening again? My mind was like a film projector, flickering back and forth between thoughts—my first deployment to Iraq twenty years ago for Desert Storm, my boyfriend Josh, my parents, my brother, my pets—then back to Josh. We had been dating only a few months, but I knew this was the person I wanted to spend my life with. We'd had to say goodbye underneath an escalator, where no one could see us. Knowing I was leaving for war, knowing I might not ever see him again, I held him tighter than I'd ever held anyone. All around us husbands and wives, boyfriends and girlfriends, hugged and kissed each other in plain sight, without secrecy, without shame. Josh and I wiped our tears dry and left our hideout in opposite directions so people didn't notice. This is the real face of "Don't Ask, Don't Tell."

A voice on the loudspeaker shot me back to the present moment: "Ladies and Gentlemen, your in-flight movie is going to be *Brokeback Mountain*." Everyone burst into laughter. I sat there, hurt and speechless. I was headed to Iraq, to live with these people for an entire year, and they were sitting here mocking me, but they didn't even know it. These people were now my family; they were the only thing I had as I left everything else behind. Words can't express the emptiness of leaving everyone you love to go to war, knowing that your new family feels this way about you (or people like you). Just the other morning, I'd had to listen to them break out in song about some guy taking it up the butt. Didn't they know there could be someone on that plane who was gay or had a gay child or gay friends? Then again, why worry when you have a law that backs you? "Don't Ask, Don't Tell" was their green light to bully me. I looked around again at all those people laughing. I felt cold and empty, and that was not from knowing I was headed off to a war.

When we landed to refuel, I got off the plane to call Josh. I told him I didn't think I could make it. He calmed me down, even though hearing his voice made me more homesick. While waiting to reboard, I saw a guy walking around snapping pictures of people. It seemed innocent enough. He was attempting to make people feel good, to get everyone's mind off of our reality. He then aimed the camera at me, and the guy next to me said, "Smile and say homo."

At that point I actually felt like God hated me. I wondered if I had done something horrible to someone and this was my karma. All these antigay things happening one right after another was like a cruel joke. I wouldn't wish this on my worst enemy. I was seconds from exploding and telling everyone that this was rude, that there might be people on the plane who had gay family members. But I didn't. I stayed quiet, just as I had for twenty years. I guess I was saving it for later.

It's not like I wasn't used to tolerating this stuff, but it was always in little doses. I would go to our battle assemblies for two days each month and come home exhausted, like I had just run a marathon dodging little hate comments. Now I was facing more than four hundred days of having to live this lie twenty-four hours a day. It is impossible to make someone who is not gay or has never been discriminated against understand what I was feeling. I'd say it's similar to white people not being able to understand what it's like to be treated differently for being black, but the analogy doesn't work because people can see your skin color, so despite whatever prejudice they have, most likely they wouldn't aim a camera in your face and say, "Smile, you nigger!" It is an awful feeling to be invisible, to have people assume you're straight, so their behavior is acceptable.

The end of December in Iraq quickly approached, and the politics were heating up in Washington. The repeal of "Don't Ask, Don't Tell" (DADT) had just been voted in. It then took from late December 2010 until mid-July 2011 for the government to determine that the repeal would have no effect on fighting forces. The government's primary concern was for the welfare of soldiers in the field (meaning straight soldiers at war), but no one was considering how the repeal would affect people like me (also at war).

The repeal date was finally set for September 20, 2011. Each day it came closer, a freedom that I could never have imagined emerged. I didn't realize how much anger had built up inside of me until it was all about to be over. One evening I watched an interview with Michele Bachmann on TV. When asked if she would reinstate DADT, without hesitation she answered, "Yes, I would." This woman sat before my eyes, never having served in the military a day in her life, saying she would ban me from serving my country. And here I was in Iraq, in the middle of a war. It was like the *Titanic* had just been saved from the iceberg, but Michele Bachmann was down in the bottom of the ship with a corkscrew. She had no explanation for her comment; she just made it a personal mission, a vendetta, to reinstate this horrible law.

I had read the stories about her husband's clinic to help people "pray the gay away." This terrified me. Could someone with such extreme intolerance and hate actually become the most powerful person in the United States of America? Where might this end? Could a KKK member also become the president? America is founded on pride in the diversity of our people. What happens when someone who leads our wonderful nation has deep-rooted hate for a particular group of people?

I woke up on the morning of September 20 and had this simple thought: I am safe. I don't have to accept anyone saying ignorant things around me anymore. I don't have to worry someone will see me holding Josh's hand anymore. I don't have to ever hide another fucking picture in my own house anymore. It was like being a POW for forty years, having someone unlock the door, then stepping outside to feel sunlight on your face. Don't get me wrong, it's not like I started waving a rainbow flag wherever I went. I just went about my day as I always had done. I was a soldier just like before, but now I was a soldier who no longer had to worry about losing his job, losing his retirement, losing everything he had worked over twenty years to build. I saw on the Internet that some people were planning on coming out instantly, but I kept thinking about what Bachmann had said about reinstating "Don't Ask, Don't Tell." I started wondering if this was just another trap for gay people. We will give you freedom, let you come out, then reinstate the ban and kick you all out. Tease you with a taste of equality and then rip it right out of your gay hands.

It must have been fate that I saw a commercial around that time on Fox News for the upcoming Republican primary debate, scheduled for September 22, 2011. The commercial said you could submit a question via video, and it just might make it into a final pool that would be aired live. It started out like a fantasy, the frightened child who envisions standing up to the bully while everyone cheers him on. Then reality set in, all the bad things that could come out of this. Finally I mustered the guts to record an anonymous video. I took my name and rank off my shirt and didn't show my face. I uploaded it to YouTube.

I didn't know if it would even get noticed. This was Fox News, after all. But people started voting on the questions, and mine lit up. It seemed that for a lot of people this was unheard of, as if gay people serving in the military were just an old wives' tale. I don't know if it was the votes or all the controversial comments that got my question noticed, but the next day I received an email from a woman who works for Google, which was sponsoring the GOP debates. She said they were considering using my question, but they didn't want me to hide my identity. I felt exposed, naked. She had my email, she knew who I was. I emailed back and told her I couldn't do that. I was not out to anyone in my unit or many people at my job back home. But that fire was still burning red hot, and I wanted an answer. I called Josh, and we talked about it. We had decided back in May that since the repeal was going to happen and they were not kicking people out, we could get married, and we had done so on my R&R. Now Josh poured gasoline on the smoldering coals when he reminded me of what would happen to us if the repeal was reinstated now that we were legally married. It was evident to me that someone had to confront the candidates and ask what their intentions would be if they held the most powerful position in the United States.

So I recorded the video showing my face. I felt so vulnerable. The question I asked (uncut) was:

Hello, I'm a soldier currently serving in Iraq, and I have a question for the Republican candidates. In 2010, when I was deployed to Iraq, I had to lie about who I was, because I am a gay soldier and I didn't want to lose my job. My question is, under one of your presidencies, do you intend to circumvent the progress that has been made with gay and lesbian soldiers in the military? Or would you continue to allow us to serve openly and *not* fear losing our jobs? Also, would you consider extending the same spouse benefits to gay and lesbian soldiers who are legally married as you do to our heterosexual counterparts? Thank you very much and have a good day.

If I was going to send it, I had basically one day until I poten-
tially would come out to everyone on national television. I
sat down with my good friend and fellow soldier Tims. I had
decided she'd be the first person I'd come out to, and I also told
her about the video I was about to send. She was very supportive
and told me she wanted to pray about it. I wasn't sure if I could
show my face. After talking to her, after talking to Josh over and
over about it, and after thinking again about what I had been
through for so many years, all that pent-up anger caused me
to hit "send." There was no taking it back. Less than one week
prior I had not planned to come out to anyone. Now this fire had
driven me to do things I never imagined. With one click of the
mouse I sealed my fate—and exposed the most personal secret
I have ever had to millions of people. What had I just done?

I decided I also owed it to Renshaw, my best buddy in Iraq,
to come out to him before this thing hit the airwaves. One thing
about DADT is that people are usually invasive about your personal life. They ask you directly to see pictures of your wife or
girlfriend. Renshaw had always been one of those people. He
used to ask if I had a Facebook page, and I'd skirt the issue. I
never added any of my coworkers or fellow soldiers to my Facebook account. If I ever thought I was at risk for being exposed
to someone who knew someone, I would unfriend them immediately. There are so many Steve Hills that I thought for sure
Renshaw wouldn't find me. But lo and behold, one day a friend
request from him popped up. I ignored it, hoping he wouldn't
say anything. But he kept pressing the issue. I told him my wife
might have accidentally blocked him. These are the kinds of
things that people don't think about. It isn't anything mean
or deliberate; it's just an innocent friend request. But to a gay
person in the closet it's a direct attack on your anonymity.

Deep down inside I was worried Renshaw would have to
explain to people why he had no idea about my being gay.
We were good friends; we had hung out and gone to the gym

together our whole time in Iraq. I felt like I needed to give him time to prepare. Not once was I really thinking about how this all would affect me. I was forced to either tell him and risk losing our friendship or not tell him and risk him feeling betrayed by me, so I told him. He said, "You're my buddy; nothing changes that." And he never treated me differently, though later he joked and said I was a really good liar because he had no idea.

I went to bed that night not knowing if my question would air. If it didn't, then I had just come out to two people. If it did, I didn't know how I was going to handle it. I set my alarm for 4 a.m. and kept thinking over and over: "Honor. Integrity. Personal courage." Those are my army values. DADT has no place within those values, but what I was about to do took all three. That question *had* to be answered. I could not go back to that life of lying.

I tossed and turned throughout the night, but at the 4 a.m. blare of my alarm I sat up in bed and turned on the TV. There it was, the debate. I could watch it live! It was like an action movie unfolding right in front of my eyes. I called Josh on Skype during the commercials. We watched for the first hour, and my question didn't come on. Part of me secretly felt relieved, thinking it might not air. Then Fox News host Megyn Kelly announced that after the break the debate would address "social issues." Could that mean me? I was on a roller coaster—that point where you're cranked up the hill, heart beating a thousand miles a minute, just going over the top, no stopping this now.

"Mr. Santorum, this next question raised a whole lot of controversy online. It comes from Stephen Hill, a soldier currently serving in Iraq."

My gut dropped out. I looked at my clock, and it was 5:19 a.m. Chow started at 5:30. If this had aired ten minutes later, thousands of people right there in Iraq would have seen it. Then I would have gotten myself into an extremely awkward situation by coming out to a bunch of people in the chow hall.

The first thing I noticed was that Fox News cut off the part directing the question to all the Republican candidates. They asked only Rick Santorum. They also cut off the second part about benefits (which I still wanted to know the answer to). And then it happened. People in the audience booed me. All the thought and preparation and courage to send it, and I was actually booed in front of millions of people on live TV. But rather than feeling anger, I instantly felt shame come over me. What had I done to deserve this? I had not seen any previous debates, so I didn't know if an audience had ever reacted like that before. But they actually booed me. My mind immediately shifted to the way Santorum answered the question. I felt a bit like a kid who gets scolded by his parents. All those negative, fearful thoughts are what prevent those of us who are oppressed from ever standing up for ourselves.

I never meant to be a gay role model, and I never thought I'd see myself being talked about on TV, in blogs, and as the subject of late-night laughs. But now you can Google "gay soldier booed," and my face and name pop up all over the place. This story is about being gay, growing up gay, joining the army, and hiding who I am. It is about discovering myself, hating myself, and eventually working up the courage to accept myself. I have written this story to inspire other gay people to be courageous and stand up for themselves and their rights. The journey reminds me of an Indiana Jones movie, where Indy has to take a leap of faith onto an invisible bridge. On September 22, 2011, I was at that bridge. I made a choice. This story is composed of all the events that led up to that choice, how I felt when I jumped onto that invisible bridge, and the fallout.

2 Don't Say Gay

Growing up there was this thing inside of me; it was so dark. I couldn't understand it. I remember feeling attraction to other boys as far back as the second grade, but it really manifested itself in the form of jealousy. I was always jealous of this one good-looking kid because he could run faster than I could. I thought that if I could run as fast as him, the feeling would go away. I also thought that if I could be as attractive as him, the feeling would go away. It took me more than twenty years to realize the feeling was attraction. I wish someone would have sat me down and said, "Hey kid, you are gay, and the feelings you have are attractions. Don't fear them because there is nothing wrong with you. Some people are attracted to women, and some are not." Maybe I wouldn't have experienced such darkness and disconnection all those years.

I am from a small town in Ohio. People from small towns can be cruel. Not intentionally, but we are not exposed to that much variety. I had some other friends in grade school, but I spent most of my time with a girl named Jenny. Something always drew me toward her. I think we had perfectly matched personalities. We would play school (who plays school?), making up fake tests and grading them. We also pretended to be in the army and played with G.I. Joe (foreshadowing?). Her dad owned a computer store, and she's probably one of the people who got me interested in computers.

I think my parents became worried that I didn't have any

other friends and that I was bonding with Jenny too much. Maybe they felt our relationship was inappropriate. They eventually told me I couldn't play with her as often, and that was devastating. Of course I know this isn't what caused me to be gay, but I also know parents sometimes blame themselves when their child comes out. I wonder if my parents think back and wonder if they shouldn't have restricted my friendship with her.

My mom often tells me that when I was growing up, she could sense something was wrong with me inside. I don't mean wrong as in being gay; I mean wrong as in this darkness I couldn't understand. There were so many instances when my depression would show itself. I have a vivid memory of sitting with my family at a Chinese restaurant and being so scared of these feelings inside that my hearing just went silent, as it often did when I was overwhelmed by my emotions. People were talking all around me, but the scene was muted. I chose to take myself out of that place, put my head down, and self-loathe. I did this a lot as a kid. My mom called me out on it and said, "What is the matter with you?" I could never tell her because I didn't understand it myself.

This makes me think about the "Don't Say Gay" bill introduced in Tennessee and Missouri. If passed, this law would have prohibited any mention of homosexuality in school. From the outside looking in, you might say, "Don't teach people how to be gay." But allowing the word *gay* to be spoken freely does not mean schools promote being gay. Making it illegal to say the word *gay* teaches gay kids to hate themselves—even more than they already do. The consequences are grave. The media has finally exposed the dangers of bullying and its link to teen suicides. But even people who survive bullying and self-loathing to eventually accept themselves as gay often waste half their lives struggling to get there. Then there are the gay people who buckle down to live a "normal life." They marry and have kids, but it's all for cover. When I finally came out, I met so many people who lived these lives. They sat in parking lots of bars and tried to meet people to fulfill their sexual urges, while their families waited for them at home.

The pressure kids face in school is enormous. People judge you by the clothes you wear, how cool you are, how tall, rich, or attractive you are, who you are friends with, who you date. I really buckled under all that pressure. The few friends I had in high school during the 1980s were an odd mix, all outcasts in our own way. We had a gung-ho wannabe marine, a very geeky dude, a kid who was socially awkward (even more than I was), and another funny guy who wanted to be in the army. With that group of friends I always felt safe because it was never about women or sex. It was about Dungeons and Dragons or video games. Most of the time I'd come home from school and play with my Commodore 64 computer. I remember my mom saying, right in front of one of her friends, "If Steve ever dates a girl, it will be a computer!" How embarrassing! But that was probably the first time that I ever thought to myself, *Wow, something might be different about me*. I had never related it to sex until she said that.

I honestly did try to date girls. I found someone I enjoyed spending time with, but she was more of a girl friend than a girlfriend. I remember taking her home after a date, and as I was saying goodnight in the car, I wanted to try to kiss her. But it wasn't a natural feeling. There was no sexual urge to do it, but society told me this was normal. So if it was normal, if I kept trying it, it would eventually work, right? We looked into each other's eyes. We slowly moved close, our lips barely touching. Then it was painfully awkward, like a scene from an *American Pie* movie. Our lips didn't hit right, her mouth was open too much, it all fell apart. I apologized and said that we could maybe try later. I think there are defining moments in a gay person's life, and for me this was one of them. We dated for a while but decided it wasn't working out. I was scared to tell my dad when we broke up because I felt like for the first time in my life I had made my parents proud by having a girlfriend.

Later in high school, I was approaching the dreaded junior prom. A girl who was a grade above me found me attractive, so we went out on a few dates, and I asked her to the prom. Meanwhile my best friend in high school was a popular, good-looking kid. His plan for prom was that I was going to lose my virginity. I was excited and nervous because I felt like I was about to receive the stamp of approval from society. We went out and bought condoms. One thing led to another, and I was ready to go. I probably could have gone through with the whole sex thing, but as irony would have it, my buddy was having so much fun at the prom that he didn't want to leave. So I got pissed off because I felt my chance at being normal slipping away. Then my date got mad at me because I was acting like an ass. We ended up fighting, and that sealed my virginity fate.

After that night I was left with my old self and this weird thing inside of me that I didn't understand. When prom came again the next year, I was in a deadlock. I didn't want a repeat of the previous year. But you have to go to prom, or you're a loser. And of course you have to have a date. One of my best female friends, Brenda, was dating someone, but since he was from another school, her boyfriend agreed to let me take her. It was a bit odd, but at least it was cover for another year.

Trust me, I have tried to be attracted to women. I remember looking for pictures of women that I could try to be attracted to. As a child I once found a picture of a woman who was a fitness model; she had crazy abdominal muscles. I couldn't believe I could be attracted to her body! *Wow! . . . I am normal!* I forced myself to try to masturbate to her picture to make myself feel normal. When people say that being gay is a choice, I always remember trying to unchoose it. People will never understand the damage done by making people think they have the ability to change something so fundamental. Later I realized my success was because she looked like a muscular man.

My brother and I had a foster sister who was attractive and popular in school. I became friends with some of her friends, particularly one girl I always joked around with in science class. She was dating a guy whom I found incredibly attractive, though I never admitted that to myself at the time. Even to this day it feels shameful to admit my attraction to men. I am dumbstruck by how much society impacts how you feel about yourself!

He was jealous of my friendship with his girlfriend, which led to some strong words and him challenging me to a fight. I had never fought anyone before. I decided that I would meet him but would try to mend things and explain that he had nothing to worry about. He was surprised when I showed up. I wasn't a particularly strong kid in high school, but he seemed nervous. Then I could see something in his eyes, like a dog sensing its domination over another dog. His nervousness changed to anger when he saw in my eyes that I didn't want to fight. I let this kid beat the shit out of me. He beat me up because of jealousy that I might steal his woman. I allowed him to beat me up because I was too attracted to him to fight back.

This wasn't the only time I was attracted to a friend's boyfriend. It happened again with a female coworker at the grocery store where I worked during high school. Her boyfriend had these great abdominal muscles, and I was just starting to work out. I still could not admit I was gay, but again I had that weird feeling that I thought was just jealousy over his abs. To this day I always wonder if that's why gay men work out so much. Maybe I wanted muscles so my feelings could be explained by competition, rather than attraction that I didn't understand. I still work out like crazy. And I often think about that.

I went through high school at a time before pornography was easily attainable, at least in my little town. So our porn involved looking at the underwear section in those silly Sears catalogs. I remember how excited I would get when the new catalogs came. But I hadn't yet accepted being gay, so if I ever masturbated, there always had to be a picture of some hot woman somewhere in the vicinity that I could also glance at to justify my arousal.

Sears led to Soloflex commercials. While staying up late to watch the music videos that used to air on Friday and Saturday nights, I saw my first Soloflex commercial. These commercials were really homoerotic, always featuring a very good-looking man with bulging muscles and oiled skin, a look that was really big in the '80s. Once I caught a glimpse of those commercials, I started seeking them out on the weekends—a tiger stalking its prey. We had just gotten a VCR, so I taped one. This was one of my first real gay acts. I remember being terrified that if someone accidently hit play, I would have to explain myself. Slowly I was turning from darkness to a secretive self-discovery, but I was terrified someone would find out. I placed the commercial all the way at the end of the tape, and I buried the evidence in a chest full of other tapes. It sounds so sinister.

While other kids were being engaged with talks about the birds and the bees, embracing their sexuality, I was hiding and suppressing mine. I wasn't trying to understand it. It was hidden in a locked dungeon, and I fed it every once in a while with a magazine to keep it at bay. I did just fine not having sex in high school. What was inside of me was way too dark to try to understand. It was something to be suppressed, not embraced. I was always ashamed and afraid of what it was, what I was.

One thing that makes being gay so hard is the loneliness. If I were black, the one thing I could count on would be that my parents would know what it's like. They would have lived it, and they could be there for me when people treated me differently. Being gay is like being an alien. You are born into something that your parents cannot relate to or sometimes even understand or accept.

People in the army were so surprised when they found out I was gay. They said time and time again, "Wow, you're a good liar." It all started with hiding those catalogs and staying up to watch those commercials. Most kids sneak around when it comes to their sexual awakening. But if parents catch them with porn or masturbating, they have "the talk." When you are gay, if parents find evidence of your sexuality, there is a chance you could lose their love. They could kick you out of the house. They could take you to counseling. This is all terrifying to a child. It's why I became a perfect liar. And I had a lifetime to practice.

As I got closer to high school graduation, I began thinking about how I'd pay for college. My parents are the type of people who would never pay for college, even if they could afford it. They always taught us that if you have to work hard for something, then you appreciate it more and perform better. I found myself getting curious about the military. My dad was in Vietnam, my brother is a police officer, and I had many other family members who were in the military. When I decided that I wanted to join the army, I really thought a lot about my dad. It was like a bonding thing, and I was very proud to follow in his footsteps. I never thought for a second that I would end up going to war, let alone going to war twice over the span of twenty years.

I started talking to recruiters. The pizza parties and food they threw at me made the army a shoo-in. I signed up for the delayed entry program in 1988, the year before I graduated high school. Shortly after I enlisted, I went to the MEPS (Military Entrance Processing Station) in Columbus to get my physical. I had a bus ticket and a hotel room. I felt like such a grown-up. Everything about the visit was pretty normal until I got to the physician. There are moments in your life that permanently scar you. A fraction of a second, one word someone says that you will hold in your memory until the day you die. This day was about to be one of them.

"You don't take it up the ass, do you?" he said.

It's funny, but I wasn't even offended at the time—because I didn't. I kept telling myself, *I am not one of them*. He was directly asking me if I was gay, but I wasn't anywhere near ready to even admit that to myself, let alone anyone else.

Graduation came and went, and not even a couple of weeks after that I found myself headed off to the army.

3 Boot Camp and Bible Study

I found out pretty early on that I would be stationed in Germany. First they shipped me off to Fort Sill in Oklahoma for basic training. It was a little challenging, but it wasn't that bad. Back then drill sergeants were allowed to cuss at you. We weren't quite in the Vietnam era, where they could hit you, but they could still rough you up a bit. It was the first time in my life that I met people from all over the world. I was from a small town, and it opened up my eyes to diversity. I got through basic training pretty uneventfully, but not without incident.

One night I was on CQ (overnight desk duty), and a guy in my platoon told me he had a secret he wanted to share with me—he was gay. Now please don't judge me; I was really in the closet. I felt sorry for the kid, but I didn't know how to react. I told him he should probably ask to leave the army. That was pre-DADT, and my rationale for giving him this advice was that I thought gay people probably were not strong enough to make it through. He eventually did tell the drill sergeant and got kicked out. Looking back, I now realize that when people are trying to understand gay people, there is an important thing they need to know. Gay people have to also learn to understand themselves. Gay people are taught by society what we are like, what we are supposed to be. Even to this day many people's first thought is that gay people are florists, decorators, hairstylists. Then we remember that they are also firefighters, soldiers, and policemen. We have all this programming that we have to unlearn.

That is why it was easy for me not to identify with that soldier. I didn't accept that I could be gay, and I also thought gay people were weak and couldn't make it in the military.

Now that I brought up DADT, let's talk about it for a second. Historically, being gay has always been a justifiable reason for expulsion from the U.S. military. In the 1970s, thanks in part to Leonard Matlovitch (more on him later), a movement to bring civil rights to gays in the military gained marginal strength. But the Department of Defense rebounded in 1981 with a formal policy stating that "homosexuality is incompatible with military service" and that gay people are subject to mandatory discharge. DADT was enacted in 1993 as a political compromise between those who sought to reverse the 1981 ban and those who sought to keep it. With DADT in place you were allowed to be here, and if you kept quiet, you could serve silently. When I first heard about it, I thought, what a victory for gay people! Little did I know this policy would be manipulated into a witch hunt.

In basic training other soldiers always told me the military put something in your food to keep you from getting an erection. Whether they did or not was a moot point: for me it was additional cover. This was the first time in my life there was no sexual pressure, no worries about keeping up an image. I just had to do my job. I was in a combat platoon that had only men in it, so I didn't have to act like I was checking out females. This was an easy life for me.

A lot of people who went to basic training with me also ended up in Germany. We had gone through so much together and had become really good friends. I went through a lot of life changes in Germany, including a religious period. Being religious gave me a chance to find a different way to hide my homosexuality. When I hear about gay clergy people, I wonder if they chose their path for the same reason, then just stuck with it.

Being religious gave me the ability to say I wasn't having sex because I was waiting for the right woman to come along.

Some days I felt like I could give all my problems to God, and he would take them away. Then there were countless nights I spent feeling really horrible about myself because of this thing inside of me. One night my depression was in full force because I realized I was becoming attracted to my friend Joel. I felt frustrated and confused, and that quickly turned to anger. I lost control of my internal rage, and in front of my roommate I smashed our metal trashcan. I then stormed out and ran to a field that was near the base. Alone and filled with sadness, I started crying. I prayed to God to change me, to make me normal. I still would not admit to myself I was gay, but there was indisputably something in me that was different from my friends.

Dave, a civilian who led our Friday-night Bible study group, took a particular interest in me. He could tell when I was going through one of my self-loathing phases (usually after I returned from praying and crying in the field). I finally sat down with him and told him I had some issues I had to work out with God. That was scary for me, because it was a level of admission. I was so guarded; even to admit I had issues put a pinhole in my airtight lie. He said, "Whatever your issue is, God still loves you."

Joel was probably one of the first crushes I had in my life. This was different: it wasn't attraction, it was more emotional. And for the first time I knew what I felt wasn't jealousy or attraction that I couldn't explain. It was deeper than that. I liked being with him, and it scared the hell out of me. Slowly I worked through my feelings and learned that I could control them. I loved him like a brother, and that eventually overcame any other attraction I had. It was a pivotal growth process for me.

I missed my family, and the Bible study group became my German surrogate family. We would share home-cooked meals after our group sessions. I even played the piano at some of those events. I have always loved playing the piano, ever since my grandpa brought an old one home from the American Legion. I had started banging on that thing when I was a kid.

I could never read sheet music, and I never had an interest in taking formal lessons, but I could always sit down and play whatever I heard. It's like being able to speak another language.

If I was ever mad, I would go play the piano. If I was happy, I would go play the piano. I think it was a kind of therapy for dealing with my childhood darkness, an escape that helped me relax. It played the same role for me in Germany. The recreation center on base had a piano, and I'd go there almost every night to play it. There was a woman who sat at the desk, and she'd chat with me whenever I came to sign out the piano.

It was getting close to Christmas 1990, and we learned that Saddam Hussein had invaded Kuwait. America was about to go to war (a war that the government never called a war), and there was talk about us being mobilized. As active duty army, I had to be ready to go to war at any time. All I had to do was throw my stuff in storage and go. Being in the active duty army, we used to tease that reservists were not real army. But over the years not only has the military called on reservists more, but at one point during the wars in Iraq and Afghanistan reservists made up *half* of everyone deployed. My second deployment twenty years later—as a reservist—was eye opening. Reservists actually have to plan for someone to take care of their pets, their house, and their bills all the time in case they are deployed. As a reservist you have to stop your life and put everything on hold (for you and everyone around you). Never again will I feel like there is a difference between reservists and active duty army. We are truly an army of one.

As soon as we got word of deployment, I went to a payphone and called my parents. It was 3 a.m. in Ohio, and here I was, not even twenty-one years old, telling them I was headed off to war. I had no idea how hard it would be for my parents to send me off to war. Going to war seemed much less dangerous to me than to the people back home. Only now do I realize that. My dad almost died of malaria when he was in Vietnam (before I was born), so I can imagine those kinds of things were running through their heads.

I decided that deployment would be a good time to start a journal. Writing in my journal was a chore at first, but later it became my best friend. Until then I'd never obligated myself to do something every single day. I had no idea what war was going to be like. I just knew that by keeping every thought I had in this journal, somehow I'd be able to share my feelings with the world. I also really wanted to keep it for my dad. I figured that if something ever happened to me, at least my thoughts would survive. I thought he would love to see what I had experienced, since he had also gone to war around twenty years earlier.

My first entry in that journal was on the plane ride over from where I was stationed in Zirndorf, Germany, to where I would serve in my first war, in Saudi Arabia.

4 Lost and Found in Iraq

The flight to Iraq seemed to take forever. I will never forget the moment I walked off the plane. I could tell I was in a part of the world where I had never been before. The air I took into my lungs had such a strange, dry smell. The air, the environment, everything felt so foreign, so dangerous. Maybe part of what I was sensing in each breath was the knowledge that I could be killed in this place so far from home.

I wrote about the air—and about everything I saw, smelled, tasted, or felt each day from that moment forward—in my journal. I was a 13 Foxtrot (a fire support specialist), which meant that my combat unit would go out and look for the enemy, then call for artillery. The artillery would sit in the back, way behind us. They had a longer range for shooting than the tanks, so they'd shoot to the coordinates we called in. We were not fighting in hand-to-hand combat; we were on a hunt-and-seek mission.

For about four months we mostly traveled. I was the driver of my vehicle, so basically all I did every day was drive. The army said that in Desert Storm we traveled more miles than we had in any other conflict. Man, I felt it. Our APC (armored personnel carrier) could go only twenty or twenty-five miles per hour, and the rumor was that it was made mostly of aluminum. I don't know whether that's true or not, but we always told people that since we had to go on the front line, it made sense for our vehicles to be cheap and destroyable. The joke was that a 13F's life expectancy in war was among the shortest.

Most nights we were mobile. We rarely stopped to set up tents for sleeping. I have funny pictures of me curled up in the shape of a ball in my driver's seat—my home for most of the war. It was winter in the desert. That meant it could get pretty cold, and rarely did our heater work on those nights. Then during the day it could get up to 130 degrees, and there was no air-conditioning. We didn't have Internet; we didn't even have iPods. My biggest pet peeve was that sand would always get into my Walkman cassette tapes and mess them up.

There was also no shower, but I'd set up a five-gallon bucket on the side of our vehicle and dig a trench so we could have a pseudo-shower. I was so proud to come up with a makeshift luxury that looking back I am reminded of how bad we had it. We had to wash our clothes in a bucket. For a toilet we'd use pits in the sand or PVC pipe that you could use like a urinal. Once we got established in a place, we would put up little boxes with screen fences around them and kerosene underneath. Anyone who went to Desert Storm will tell you how fond they were of "shit burning" detail. I remember running out of water a few times and having to use my bathing water to brush my teeth.

I look back at that war and think, how did I do that? I don't want to sound like one of those old folks who say, "When I was young, I had to walk thirty miles through the snow to school." But in reality we never really had a home. We never stopped. We traveled for months, moving closer and closer to the enemy. It wasn't as rough as troops had it in Vietnam, but it was a lot rougher than we have it now.

Every day I wrote in my journal. I also wrote letters home, but due to the mail I wouldn't get a response for months at a time. It was hard to write back and forth because both of you would forget what you had been talking about in your last letter. Now we have email. One of the people who wrote me the most was Pete, a close friend from childhood. He would handwrite a really long letter with lots of pages, then even decorate the outside of the envelope by coloring an American flag on the back. I think about how people don't take the time to do things like that anymore. Everything is an ecard or an evite. Pete was always creative. I later discovered Pete was gay.

We also had lots of "dear soldier" mail. So at mail call, if you didn't get anything, you might receive a letter from a child in school. One day I opened up a letter and thought a child had written it because it was so hard to read. But I later realized that my grandfather (on my dad's side) had written it. I'd had no idea that he really couldn't write. When my dad found out about that letter years later, he almost cried. He told me that he had never gotten a letter from Grandpa the whole time he was in Vietnam. I think this was because Grandpa was embarrassed, so he had Grandma write the letters. But Grandpa decided that *he* wanted to write this letter. That was very touching to me. My grandma went on and on about how important it was for him to write that letter to me on his own. I think having his first grandchild at war changed his embarrassment to motivation.

My mother is a very strong woman. When I called her from Germany to tell her I was getting deployed, she said, "We will be fine; I am not worried." All of her letters to me sounded strong, so I really relied on her strength while I was deployed. After being in Iraq for about a month without being able to call home, we were finally told we could use the phones. Keep in mind that with the delay in writing and receiving letters, your family never knew if you were okay. There could be a knock on the door at any time. They drove us out to a remote site with AT&T tents and satellites. The lines were huge. When I got closer, it suddenly hit me that for the first time I could tell my family I was okay, and they could actually hear my voice. I instantly started getting nervous and homesick.

I picked up the receiver, and the operator asked for the number. I had butterflies in my stomach. My mom answered, and it sounded like she had been crying, but it was 3:30 in the morning there, so she may have been half asleep. The operator said, "This is AT&T, and I have a collect call from . . ." This strong woman, whom I had seen cry only when her mother died, burst out in tears and screamed. This was when I realized she wasn't the tough person she made herself out to be. Hearing their voices felt so good. When my time was up, I felt like someone was taking my life away. Hanging up the phone was one of the hardest things I've ever had to do.

Besides my parents and brother back home I had no ties to anyone. Joel, whom I had lost touch with while in Iraq, used to tell me about spouses in Germany who cheated on their deployed husbands. I can't tell you how many relationships I saw the demise of in Iraq. A lot of my fellow soldiers were going through horrible divorces or breakups. I will never forget a man who killed himself in Desert Storm because his wife left him. That was one of my first exposures to suicide.

Fast-forward to September 22, 2011, when Rick Santorum answered my question by saying, "Sex has no place in the military." I beg to differ. In both 1990 and 2011 I watched someone kill himself over relationship issues. I saw people constantly distracted because of a divorce back home or relationship woes. I watched people get sent home for inappropriate sexual conduct in the military. Rape is a big concern when soldiers are deployed. We constantly watch sexual harassment videos and receive training. Mr. Santorum needs to check his facts.

Being young and free of relationship woes didn't mean I wasn't in need of some R& R. The army had a chartered cruise ship, the *Cunard Princess*, in Bahrain. Soldiers in good standing could be entered into a lottery system for a three-day stay on the ship. Up to then I had never won anything in my life, but out of the whole battalion only one other soldier and I were selected to go. We flew in a Chinook out of the combat zone in Iraq. The ship went nowhere, but it was a place where soldiers could have a few drinks and fraternize around members of the opposite sex. I wasn't interested in either, but I appreciated having a second chance to call home on the ship, and I was hopeful that I'd find a piano somewhere on board. I would often daydream about being able to play the piano while I was in Iraq. I needed that escape. The ship also had swimming, and the food was crazy! I took pictures of it to make everyone jealous when I got back to my unit in Iraq.

Unfortunately, the supper I ate on board my first night gave me food poisoning. I had never been sick like that before; I felt like I was going to die. The soldier who had come with me took me to the ship's doctor. But my illness just wasn't going away, so they took me off the ship to a local hospital. I am not sure where the ball was dropped, or who really dropped it, but somehow I was about to fall through the cracks. My friend ended up leaving me in the hospital because our R&R time was up, and he had to catch a flight back to our unit. I couldn't go: I was too sick to travel. So I stayed in that hospital.

The moment it dawned on me that I might be in trouble was the first time I attempted to eat. I showed the civilians working my military ID, and they said, "We don't accept that here." This was not good. I was somehow shifted to a non-military-led operation. As a PFC (private first class) I had no money. I had to find people who could help me find food. And I really needed to find the U.S. military folks. I was twenty years old and lost in Iraq. This was back at a time when the army wasn't so great about tracking people. Nowadays it's a lot different; ID cards and computers track all of a soldier's movements in theater. Our non-computer-laminated ID cards were not tracked in any way. I found some British troops who took me in and fed me. They were great guys. I stayed with them for a while, learned some new card games. I told them my story, and they couldn't believe it. They said they would try to help me find my way back to the U.S. troops.

They put me on a vehicle, and we headed for a marine base.

I felt a little safer and less lost once I found the marines. My first impression of the marines was funny. I witnessed two of them in a fistfight outside a chow hall. But some of them took me in and took care of me. They hooked me up with meals and eventually connected me with an army unit. The first person I talked to asked what unit I was with.

"HHB 2/1 FA," I said. He didn't know it. "Out of Zirndorf, Germany," I said. He still had no clue who that was. I started getting nervous, realizing how lost I actually was. "First Armored Division," I said. Nothing. He just shook his head, trying to make a connection with someone he knew.

I kept going up the echelons until he could figure out where to send me. It had now been more than two weeks, and nobody knew where I was; I was AWOL. A lot of those memories are blurry; I just remember I had to scrounge around to get fed. And of course I wrote about all of it in my journal.

Finally I was introduced to a soldier wearing our seventh core patch, a lieutenant colonel. I was so nervous to talk to him. I was only a PFC. I was also afraid I would be in trouble for getting lost. I walked up to him and told him my incredible story. He couldn't believe what he heard. He immediately took me out and bought me a meal—a burger and fries (it's funny how some details in life make such an impact). He arranged to get me on a flight back to our rear detachment in Saudi Arabia. The main body at that time was moving out of Iraq, so the detachment radioed them and told them I had been found.

What controversy I caused! I had to make statement after statement, and I know some heads rolled because of that mess. It's so funny how clueless you are as a PFC. Being a major now, I realize the terror I probably caused our leadership. Once the unit was close enough, they drove me out by Humvee, so I could drive my own vehicle into Saudi with the rest of the unit. SFC Harper's first reaction was to smack me on the head. He was a great guy, from a town that was close to my hometown; he was like my dad. I think his reaction came from relief that I was okay. When I was deployed, my mom used to call his wife all the time to talk, and somehow that made them both feel better.

The actual war progressed very quickly, though it didn't feel like it at the time. The ground battle lasted for eighty hours. It was pretty intense, and I barely slept that whole time. It was raining the day we went in. Rain is sporadic in the desert, but when it does rain, it pours! I saw people who were injured (mostly from the artillery we used), people missing limbs, people severely burned, and people who were dead. It's odd, but none of that really disturbed me. Then one night something incredible happened, and it rattled me more than anything else I had experienced up to that point.

It was late, and we were in battle. I've explained how artillery works: we called in a coordinate, and artillery fired. Then we basically guessed how far to the left of target we were and called a coordinate a certain number of degrees to the right. Then fired again. Then took half that distance and aim back to the left, until we hit the target. Of course that was the way we did it back then. Now we have fancy technology to do all that manual work. All of a sudden there was a huge explosion off to *our* left. I'd never seen anything like it: a big swirling fireball. If I wasn't so terrified by it, I would have thought the way it looked at night was beautiful. The next thing I knew, I saw another big explosion on the right. *They were homing in on us.*

That was the first time my life I thought I might actually die. I ducked into my driver's hatch, which was really like my bedroom. I even had photos of my family taped there. I felt like a sitting duck, waiting for the final explosion, when I happened to look up at a picture of my brother and his girlfriend. All those years of hiding who I was, being scared of it, and not admitting or understanding it *stopped right then*. My whole life had been fake. And if I were to die, I would have never been honest with myself, never let myself love another person. I was so scared, and I felt like I was going to die alone. I promised myself, in those couple of seconds until the next artillery shell came in, that if I made it back, I was going to finally start living my life for myself. I hadn't made the decision to come out of the closet to the world. But that was the moment I came out to myself. The darkness was finally exposed for what it was, and I was ready to face it.

We learned over the radio that the artillery impacting all around us *was* us. The U.S. troops were shooting at what they thought was the enemy: friendly fire. There was a lot of maneuvering and flanking, and I guess all that flanking confused people. Luckily that last blast never happened, or I might not be here today.

It wasn't very long before we found out that the war (which was never a war) had been declared over. And we found out we would be coming home. But back then five months seemed like ten years. When you can't talk to your family and friends, time slows down. That war took a toll on me. I decided to get out. I would go into the inactive reserves and finish college.

Sitting on the plane back to Germany, I wrote in my journal, just as I had on the plane that first brought me over and every day thereafter. When we landed, we boarded a bus to the parade celebrating our return. We had to wear our desert battle dress uniforms (BDUs) and leave our belongings on the bus so we could march in for the families and local Germans, who were cheering for us. When I came back to the bus, my bag was gone. Someone must have wanted the Walkman and Gameboy in it, but they also wound up stealing my journal. You can lose a house in a fire, but if you lose photographs, they can never be replaced. This was probably the worst loss I'd ever had. My memories and experiences were gone. Now they are kept alive only by an aging memory that every day forgets more and more of the details.

I often wonder what the thief did with my journal. Sometimes in bookstores I look around for *A Soldier's Journal* or another title like that. Most likely the person threw it away, discarding a significant portion of my life. Though I didn't write about being gay, I did write a lot about my feelings. I would love to be able to go back and read that. I fantasize about it. I think so much would make sense now that I know who I am. I was trying to comprehend death and loss and trying to balance that with the deep loneliness and regret I felt for lying to myself my whole life. I wonder how many other soldiers have come to terms with their sexuality while at war. Here I was not even old enough to drink alcohol, dealing with things I had never seen before (death), dealing with my sexuality, and documenting the entire process—and in a blink it was gone.

We went through all of the ceremonies and headed back to Pinder Barracks (my home away from home). Once we received permission to get our belongings, people bum-rushed the storage facility to get their TVs. Some people went right to the phones; others got a pass and went out on the town. I had only one thing on my mind. I had a craving, I missed it so much. With the loss of my journal still a fresh wound, the first thing I did was go back to that old recreation center. The minute the woman behind the desk saw me, she started to cry and gave me a big hug. As much as I used to play that piano, I think I owned stock in it. I signed the piano out that night and played it like never before. I played for hours and hours. I had never fallen asleep on a piano while I was playing it, but that night I did. And it was wonderful.

My military time in Germany soon came to an end. We flew to Delaware, then took a cab to the facility where we could outprocess. Finally I got a flight back to Columbus. Just recently my grandma found the videotape my family took of my homecoming at the airport. I love that video; it speaks volumes. We drove back home and stayed up most of the night talking. I was so happy to be in my real home again. In the window I noticed a flag with the names of everyone deployed, which my parents had cut out from our hometown newspaper.

There was also one of those cheesy little Christmas-candle lights, which I quietly turned out after my parents went to bed. The next morning I woke up when my mom screamed, "Who turned out my light!" She explained that when I left, she turned that little light on and vowed to leave it on, day and night, the entire time I was gone. She felt that as long as it was on, I would be okay. The funny thing is, she couldn't turn it back on after I turned it off. It was like my guardian, my protector while I was at war. And I guess I didn't need it anymore—at least not for another twenty years.

5 Pink Triangles

I enrolled at The Ohio State University not even a month after returning from Germany. I moved in with John, a high school buddy and my best friend. We had grown up together, and now he had a year's head start on me in college. John joined the army years later (because of a motivation to serve his country after 9/11) and eventually went on to serve two tours in Iraq. But back in 1991 he was my roommate, and I still remember when the army shipped my stuff home from Germany. It was like Christmas for me and John, with all my stuff arriving by freight in one day. We furnished our college apartment with my stuff, which was a notch above junk, although to college students it was a gold mine.

John always wanted to go to the campus bars, but I always tried to come up with an excuse not to go. Even though I'd had an epiphany in Iraq about living my life for myself, this would take some time and getting used to. I was not ready to jump into a gay lifestyle just yet. I was always afraid something would happen, or a woman would be interested in me, and I'd be called out for being gay. One night we were out at a local campus bar, listening to Chris Logsdon, a singer who played the guitar and took requests on the fly. We were having a great time, and one woman was getting really plastered. John was a little tipsy himself, so he didn't notice what was going on. She got drunker and drunker and started pointing to me. I felt really nervous; if John caught a glimpse of this, he would definitely want me to talk to her. Sweating like crazy, I acted like I didn't see her. Then her friends started laughing and pointing to her, then to me. They were getting more and more suggestive. I freaked out. I told John I was sick and we had to get out of there.

Years later, after I had come out to John, I told him that story. We were laughing about it, and all of a sudden he hit me and said, "Why didn't you tell *me* about her?" Apparently I had wasted the optimal situation every straight twenty-year-old in the world would want to be in.

When John wasn't dragging me to bars, we hung out and rented movies. One night he really wanted to rent Madonna's *Truth or Dare*. I had no desire to see it, but being a good sport, I agreed. Halfway through the movie I decided to go to bed because I thought the movie was dumb, but then I saw the scene where Madonna dares two guys to kiss. I had never seen anything like that in my life. It was exhilarating. Later that night I lay in bed for hours thinking about it. I waited for John to go to sleep, then got up and searched for that spot on the video. I rewound and watched that scene over and over again. That moment confirmed for me deep down inside that I was gay, no matter how much I didn't want it to be true, and that I was never going to escape it.

One of my classes freshman year was a sociology class. The professor invited someone from the Gay and Lesbian Student Alliance, a guy named Marc, to be a guest speaker in class. Nothing could have prevented me from attending class that day. I was so curious to actually see another real gay person (not on TV, but in person). He was attractive, but he wasn't at all what I had expected. I thought he would be queeny or maybe dark and sinister. But I saw a typical college student who was not only comfortable with his sexuality but made being gay seem normal. He spoke to the group, and I couldn't believe people were not stoning him. In my hometown one of the stories printed in an April Fool's Day edition of the newspaper said that the town was having a gay rights parade. And that was supposed to be a joke. So this level of acceptance was unheard of for me.

I eventually worked up the nerve to talk to Marc. I told him I thought I might be gay. I couldn't believe those words actually came out of my mouth. It was hard but so liberating. After that night in Iraq, and after the *Truth or Dare* kiss, I could finally admit it to myself. But to admit it to another human being was another story. Marc invited me to attend Gay and Lesbian Student Alliance meetings and said to let him know if I ever needed a friend or wanted to hang out.

I kept thinking about that, day and night, for about a week. I wasn't ready to go to a gay group. But I gathered up the courage to invite Marc to an AC/DC concert movie. He accepted, but I think he hated it. I felt bad that he wasn't enjoying the movie, so we left early and went to get coffee. Talking to him that night helped me in a lot of ways. For the first time in my life I felt a bond with someone who could understand what I was going through. I had found another alien who spoke my language, something my own parents couldn't do. When I dropped him off at his house, I was afraid he would try to kiss me or make some kind of move. It's funny how homophobic society can make you, even toward your own people.

Marc called me a couple of times and invited me to join him and his friends at a gay bar called the Garage. I kept making up excuses not to go; I just wasn't ready for that yet. But I wanted so badly to see this place and be social for once in my life. So at 8:30 on a Wednesday night, when none of my roommates were home, I got the courage to look up the address and hop in my car by myself. My heart was beating a thousand times a minute as I drove there. I sat in the parking lot for an hour and watched people go in and out. I kept thinking I would see a bunch of creepy people in leather. But they all seemed normal. I took a deep breath and finally got out of my car. This was a big step for me.

When I walked in, I got a couple of stares. I kept thinking, "My God, there are only twenty of us in Columbus," not realizing it was dead because it was still early on a weeknight. I ordered a soda, and the bartender took my money.

"Here you go, honey," he said as he handed me my change.

I was freaked out that he called me "honey." It was like I was looking for signs to make me reconsider coming out. I also remember being scared to drink from the straw because I thought I could get AIDS from that. Back then there wasn't nearly as much HIV information available as there is today. And like I said, society had programmed me to hate and fear gay people. This is the same hate I am trying to tear down by writing this book, by showing people how innocent this process is and how dangerous all the self-loathing is. Knowing how terrified I was of these "gay people," can you imagine how much I hated myself all those years for thinking I might be one of them? It's no wonder people kill themselves over this. I sat there and awkwardly sipped my soda and didn't talk to anyone. I left when my glass was empty.

I eventually took Marc up on his offer to come to the group meetings. At that time the Gay and Lesbian Student Alliance was still referred to as a support group. Through it I started making friends and gaining confidence. I don't think it necessarily made it easier to be gay, but it made me hate myself a little less. I knew that I was different, but for the first time in my life I found out that there were other people like me.

Most people think coming out is just making some declaration that you are gay. It is much more complex than that. First it is realizing what you are and who you are. Then it is countless hours spent learning to unlearn the self-hatred that has been programmed into you by society. Eventually you find others and realize you are not alone. This helps you hate yourself less. And if you make it this far, the last step is accepting and even eventually being proud of yourself. There are quite a few hurdles to getting there. Unfortunately there are a lot of people who never make it.

During college I had to do an internship. I rotated among different organizations and worked in different positions as a dietitian. This was a critical part of my life: I was trying to come to terms with who I was and struggling with my sexuality. During my rotation at Franklin County's MRDD (mental retardation/developmental disabilities) facility (which has now dropped the MR and uses the more accepted DD title) I worked at a school full of children with developmental disabilities. I remember meeting with some of the parents of these kids. I tried to put myself in their place and understand how hard it must be to have the additional stress of raising a child with a disability. The profound thing for me was that the parents I met with didn't blink an eye. They were so loving and nurturing to their children, and even though their situation seemed stressful to me, they handled it with the utmost grace. It really made me start to think that a true loving parent would love you no matter what. This was where my courage to try to come out to my family started.

One day I went into the lunchroom at the school, and it was filled with children who had disabilities. Out of the corner of my eye I happened to see a little girl who was trying to eat, but she didn't have the motor skills to even get one morsel of food into her mouth. She just kept slopping food down the front of her dress. I felt so bad for her; I couldn't imagine being born with a disability and trying to cope. But when I looked at her, she sent the biggest smile in my direction; she was so happy. It was like the whole world felt sorry for her, but she didn't need their pity; there was nothing wrong with her. I left the room and cried. I felt like the biggest piece of shit in the world to ever think I had troubles or problems that would cause me to be "depressed." That little girl was my greatest teacher that day. Happiness is the absence of feeling sorry for yourself. And by God I realized that if she didn't feel sorry for herself, then I had no right to ever feel sorry for myself. That little girl changed my life. I owe a lot of who I am today to her, and she will never know that.

After that experience I had a new outlook. I started to feel like I wanted to share my secret, like I was willing to take the risk of losing my parents' love to do so. One weekend, not long after I met Marc and his friends, I went home to visit my parents and my brother, Tommy. My brother had been my best friend growing up, maybe because of my shyness with other people. Of course we fought from time to time, but we had always been close. I was resting in bed when Tommy came in and lay down beside me. I can't remember our whole conversation, but I do remember that I started to feel the darkness come over me again. Before it would have caused me to shut down and not say anything. But this time was different. I started crying, and Tommy asked what was wrong. I said I had a lot of problems and wished I could tell someone. He kept saying, "Hey, you can tell me."

I really had no intention of coming out during this visit home, but before I knew it, I blurted out, "I'm not like you. I have tried, but I just can't. I think I might be gay."

The cat was out of the bag, and I couldn't take it back. It was like popping the cork on a Champagne bottle—years and years of building up pressure, then one motion and it's opened forever. He hugged me. He seemed surprised but not like he'd stopped loving me. The next day I drove back to my apartment in Columbus. I had planned to try to get up the courage to talk to my parents, but I really couldn't. *One step at a time* is what I kept thinking.

A couple of days later the answering machine in my apartment was blinking. I clicked it, like I had a million times before, but this time the message stopped my heart.

"Steve, it's Mom. Tommy told us what you told him; please give me a call."

I had never in my life felt so exposed, so vulnerable, so open. I started to cry. I couldn't tell from the tone of my mom's message if they were mad, or if they were okay, or if that was it—I would never be allowed home again. When you come out, it's like being on trial for murder; you just wait for your verdict.

I was terrified to call, but I had to face this. Later I found out that my brother got upset and didn't know how to handle what I had told him, because he left my parents' house and went to my grandma's house for a couple of days. He came back and told my parents what it had taken me twenty years to work up the courage to tell him. Fingers trembling, I dialed the number. My mom picked up, and then my dad also got on the line. Mom said something to the effect of, "Tommy told us what you said, and I don't appreciate that you told him and didn't come to us." To this day she probably doesn't understand how hard it was for me to even tell my brother. I started trying to explain something to my parents that I was only starting to understand myself. My dad said, "Maybe you are just bisexual." In his mind it was like there were levels of gayness. Sadly, society had programmed my parents just like everyone else. My dad thought that if I was bisexual, at least there would still be hope because I would like girls.

Recently I was telling my mom I was planning to write this book, and she provided more insight on that day. She told me one of her first thoughts: "I was scared you would molest children." It's amazing how little any of us understood. I myself had stood outside the gay bar staring for hours at the people who walked in, as if I were looking for something that would make me decide to cancel the whole thing (like I could).

After I hung up with my mom, I felt scared and isolated. I felt a gut-wrenching loneliness. I pulled the covers over my head, and my cat pushed her way through. She was purring really loudly, as if she could tell I was upset. I felt comforted by her, and that was the moment I understood what unconditional love is. It comes so easily from animals. But people? Not so much. People often make fun of the way gay people love (or overlove) their pets. I wonder if that's because our pets are safe for us, something we can pour our emotion into and know it will be returned.

I know my parents love me unconditionally, but at that moment I was questioning everything, and it sucked. Things were uncomfortable between my parents and me for a while after that. A couple of weeks later my mom and I started calling each other again. I slowly started including details about my life that I never had before, and I think this helped fill in the gaps for her. Unconditional love prevailed, and she made an effort to reduce the tension by coming to Columbus for a visit, just the two of us. We went to see the film *The Bodyguard*. At one point she asked me if I thought Kevin Costner was cute. That was super weird, not only because I didn't but also because my mom had asked me that question. Sometimes I think it is as hard to accept acceptance as it is to give it. At least that was the case for me.

My mom and I had a wonderful night. We went to OSU, walked around, and visited the Oval, the big lawn in the middle of campus. I wanted to introduce her to my first boyfriend, but I don't think either one of us was ready for that. Recently my mom told me that when she came home that night, my dad asked how I was doing. She replied, "If you want to know how he is doing, then you need to call him." I guess my brother asked the same thing and got the same answer.

The next time I spoke to my dad, he made a bisexual comment again. I tried to explain that it doesn't work that way. He then said something like, "Are you sure? Before you choose this lifestyle . . ." I told him that the only choice I had made was not to lie to him anymore. I think that made a big difference to him. He was trying hard to show his support the best way he could. He told me that he had met a lesbian at an AA meeting, even shaken her hand. I know that comment makes him sound like a horrible person, someone who was proud of himself for shaking a hand, but for him this was a big step toward learning to love and accept me.

My parents are the greatest people I know. We are all ignorant about things we don't have any experience with. Everyone deserves a chance to grow, and my parents would soon evolve into my strength. My adoptive grandmother had a problem with me being gay, which caused a lot of friction between her and my mom. Eventually the constant tension from comments my grandmother made about me being gay resolved with my mother telling her, "If you cannot love my children equally, then you can fuck off; I don't want you in our lives." That moment was a real testimony to my mother's love for me.

I know it's harder for older generations to understand gay people. I know they were raised in homophobic, racist times. But one thing I don't buy is the argument, "I grew up like that, so I can't change." You may be able to plead ignorance because of your upbringing, but you can always choose to leave the past and start living in the present. I think America is starting to realize this now in 2014. Younger generations see LGBT issues as the civil rights struggle of their time.

My relationship with that set of grandparents to this day has been very stifled. They tolerate me, but I have never received acceptance from them. It has taken me my whole adult life to realize that I don't need their acceptance, tolerance, or approval. I just found out they are both in poor health. Now I know we will never reconcile, and they will take that hate to the grave—hate over whom I choose to love.

My other grandparents were very different. My father's mother didn't even blink an eye, though my grandfather remained quiet. I felt awkward around him the last years of his life, but honestly I don't know if that was him or me. One thing I learned after coming out to the entire world is that sometimes we create or expect things to be awkward, so we get overly sensitive. Once I had asked my question at the debate, it was almost impossible not to think people were looking at me differently. I would sit down to breakfast and swear that soldiers at the next table were talking about me. Were they? Who knows, but I know that it's easy to anticipate and perceive negativity.

When my father's father passed away, I stood up and spoke at his funeral about that letter he wrote me in Iraq. I told everyone there that I was the first one in my family to graduate from college, that I was getting a master's degree, and that I had taken dozens of English and composition courses, but nothing I could ever write would be as articulate or as powerful as the words my grandpa had sent me in that letter: "I love you," written in such an illegible script. My education and degree could produce nothing to match that. "I love you back, Grandpa," I said as I laid him to rest. My grandmother gave me their wedding band since I was the oldest grandchild.

Eventually I felt like I could start coming out to my friends. It's such a scary thing because you feel like there's a chance you could lose each person you tell. I decided to start with John, my best friend. I came out to his girlfriend first to see how she thought he would react. Secretly I was hoping she would tell him. Courage is not something that develops overnight. I eventually told him over the phone, and he seemed cool. I always wondered if she said something. My other roommate was a little less accepting, but he was okay. We lived in a duplex, and I was good friends with my neighbors, so I eventually came out to them too. One of my friends, Gina, was so funny and accepting: she told me once that she wished she could become a lesbian because of the problems she had dating certain men. It was a joke then, but at the time I think she really felt that way.

I look back at this time in my life and laugh. Imagine you have been locked up in a prison for years, never allowed to watch TV. Then all of a sudden you are freed and given unlimited cable access on a seventy-inch flat-panel high-definition TV. You'd flip from channel to channel, amazed at how many choices you have at your fingertips. It's so easy to go overboard. The same was true for my newfound access to my identity. I plastered a bumper sticker on my car that said, "Homophobia is a social disease." The more people I came out to, the more confidence I gained. I had rainbow bracelets and necklaces. I went through a "teenage-girl" phase and put up posters in my room of shirtless men. It was a terribly gaudy point in my life.

I think of that today, and I know I was living in a bubble. It seemed like the world around me was gay friendly, but this was the mid-1990s. It was far from an accepting time, especially in Ohio. I go back and look through our college paper, and I can't believe people wrote the editorials they did about gay people. But I had found a community that accepted me, and that created a false sense of security. This false sense of security was especially evident in times like the elections of 2004, when a majority of states voted to make gay marriage illegal (more on that later).

Maturity manifests itself in many different aspects of your life—relationships, employment, and social settings. Personal maturity for gay people usually doesn't come until we accept ourselves. Some of us cycle in and out of relationships because we never learned how to date. Being fickle is normal, but for gay people it often happens in our adult lives rather than our teenage years. We never got to go through that phase when we were young. It also doesn't help that society taught us that we are bad. If you feel like nothing you do will gain acceptance, you stop caring about following societal norms. It is ironic that many people mock gay people for not being in committed long-term relationships, but those same people advocate against us being allowed to marry.

Another symbol I plastered all over everything during this phase was the pink triangle. It was popular at the time, usually with the slogan "Silence = Death" in the foreground. Sounds cool enough, right? We now live in a world where many people feel like they make a difference by clicking "like" or "share" on Facebook; back then it was sticking a sticker on your backpack or your car. One night I started reminiscing about the army, Desert Storm, and Germany, so I pulled out some old photos. I stumbled upon one that I had taken during my visit to the Dachau Nazi death camp—a photo of a work uniform with wooden shoes that I had been particularly fascinated with during that visit. When I saw that picture again, I literally dropped to the floor. That uniform included a pink triangle. Everything in my brain suddenly connected: the persecution of people, senseless death, hate, all of it. That moment awakened the sleeping activist within me.

This picture made me feel like I finally understood my place in history. For the first time in my life it seemed like maybe the purpose of this darkness inside of me was a drive to understand gay history. I saw the uniform of someone who had to die for who he was. I knew that Nazi camps affected Jewish people, but that's when I realized that persecution of gay people is easily missed, our discrimination easily dismissed. Once I saw that uniform again, the Holocaust became just as real for me as it is for a Jewish person whose grandpa was killed in those camps. People were killed for being gay. I am gay, and that could have been me.

This photo also caused me to reflect on how easy it is for the masses to condone terrible judgment. Today it's mostly a universal belief that suppressing a person's civil rights is wrong. Yet in 2012 half of the people in the United States still thought it was okay to suppress my civil right to marry the person I love. And why should it end there? Why not say I shouldn't be able to vote (North Carolina is a perfect example) or drink from the same fountain as straight people? When HIV was first discovered, it was evident that the suffering of gay people wasn't a priority. Research funding for HIV became a priority only after the Reagan administration discovered the disease also affected straight people. To turn your back on a suffering people is not much better than to actually cause the suffering. The slogan of the pink triangle is right: "Silence = Death." History is important; telling our story is important.

At that point in my life I was still navigating the ups and downs of relationships. One day I was in front of my apartment, upset because I was fighting about something with my boyfriend. We were not in a good place. Someone saw us arguing, came over, and yelled, "You fucking faggots." It was a double whammy—on top of the stress of the relationship, I had never been called a faggot. I just ignored it, but the hurt lasted quite a while. It also reminded me point blank that the kind of hate that fueled the Holocaust still exists. I started to realize that I was living in a bubble when that happened.

The process of coming out affects so many levels of your life, including your job. The irony is that this process isn't necessarily initiated by you. Some argue that gay people flaunt their lifestyle, or put it "out there," when many times they are just avoiding situations that arise because of others. One of my part-time jobs in college was in the purchasing department at E. I. DuPont. I wasn't "out" at work. One of my coworkers, Jerry, was gay, and I always worried that he might find out about me. The irony is that Jerry could have been an ally, but that deep-rooted homophobia always made me think he would have other intentions. I became friends with a woman at DuPont who had pictures of her family on her desk, including a picture of a really attractive man who turned out to be her son. I always wondered if that was my motivation for befriending her. She had three kids and was really bitter because her husband had left her for another man. She started dating another man, but then he dumped her because he was bisexual. This woman had some luck, huh? She wasn't done yet. She started to grow fond of me. I wasn't ready to come out, but that was awkward. Later I decided to come out to another female friend, Kelly, who worked there. Jerry had always flirted and said little suggestive things, but after I came out to him, he became slightly more distant.

Another college job I had was working in food service at a hospital. One day a cart fell down on me and cut my face. I had blood gushing out of my face, and my eyes were swollen so big I couldn't see out of them. The doctor said I was lucky because if the cart had hit me a smidge to the left or right, I could have lost my eyesight. My parents came down to Columbus, and I went back home with Mom while Dad followed us in my car.

When we got home, my dad was all red in the face and looked really mad. "Some son-of-a-bitch winked at me," he said. It was because of my "Homophobia is a social disease" bumper sticker. That still cracks me up when I think about it.

I worked at the hospital with a guy named Vernon, who also was in my chemistry class. Later someone told me he always knew I was gay. Usually you could tell when someone knew. Not Vernon. He was one of the only people in my life who didn't treat me differently. We became such good friends that he moved in and became a roommate. He would criticize my wardrobe, so it seemed like we were stereotypical, but in reverse. He would go to gay bars with me and hit on women all the time. His scheme was to pretend he was gay and convince women that he wanted to try to have sex with a woman. He seemed to be very successful doing that.

Vernon had lost his dad when he was very young. He didn't really know his father, but he idolized him. Vernon's mom would come down and visit us, and since she knew I was gay, she decided to share the deep secret with Vernon that his dad had been gay. Vernon's dad had been honest with his mom about his sexuality but chosen to live his life with her and raise Vernon. To add insult to injury, Vernon's dad had developed cancer but didn't get treatment because he was very religious and the church he belonged to didn't believe in hospitals or doctors. They believed everything that happened was God's will. Vernon's whole life suddenly came crashing down because someone he had always looked up to was a complete mystery to him.

This impacted Vernon so much that he actually attempted to see if he might be gay. He tried to be attracted to men. It was the weirdest role reversal I had ever seen. I watched him go through this phase, and I finally sat him down and said, "You are not gay, and that is okay." It was one of the strangest moments in my life—a gay guy trying to convince a straight guy he was not gay and not to feel like he had to try it because he admired his dad.

# **6** Just Be You

When I was a freshman at OSU, some religious group presented a seminar by a group that claimed they could help you find God and heal your homosexuality. I decided to go. I was very religious for a significant period of my life, and of course somewhere in the back of my mind was the thought, what if I could change and be straight and have a wife and a family? At times I would still get a little sad thinking that I would never have a family. Of course today we have lots of role models. We see gay families with children. But we didn't have that back then.

I went in skeptical but tried to keep an open mind. The speaker went on and on about how he used to be gay, but through prayer God had healed him. I was intrigued. What had he said to God that worked? I was on my knees crying out loud in a field with nothing between God and me but the stars on a clear night. What had this guy said that was different? I approached him after the talk was over. I pretty much went for the jugular and said, "So when you say you are not gay, you mean to tell me you have no more attraction to men? When you see a hot man, it doesn't do anything for you anymore?" He answered, "No, I still am attracted to men; I just don't act on my attraction."

Then the fangs came out, and I lashed at him. "Then you are a motherfucker for sitting up there and lying to all these people," I said. "Do you know how badly some of these people hate themselves? They pray, and they are a thread away from deciding to end their life. They feel like a failure. You sit up here and lie to them and tell them you successfully changed. So now they hate themselves *worse* and feel more like a failure. If one of them takes their life because of you, I hope you live every day and remember what you caused. You are an awful *gay* human being." He looked surprised and really didn't say anything back. I hope my words sunk in.

I know lots of back and forth goes on about being gay and what that means in religion. I know there are verses in the Bible that condemn being gay. There are also Bible verses that condone slavery. So I guess you can argue back and forth about the validity of different verses. But my friend at DuPont once said something to me that resonated more than any religious argument ever could. She said, "Steve, I just do not believe that God would hate someone for loving someone."

The night of the "change your sexuality" seminar, I came home and slept like a baby, not only because I gave that guy hell for misleading all those people but also because I felt like I wasn't a failure. I felt like God wasn't ignoring me and listening to other people. I started feeling like maybe, just maybe, my purpose on this earth was to be exactly who I am. It felt good. One of my favorite shirts of all time said: JUST BE YOU. It was marketed to the gay community, but that message can apply to a lot of situations in life. When I stood up and asked my question to the Republican candidates, I did exactly that. Just be you.

When I talk to people about being gay, I always hear the "it's a choice" argument. I have gotten into many disagreements about this. Being gay, you *do* have a choice. I could choose to suppress my feelings and live a life without a relationship or sex. (Rick Santorum said that to me directly.) Or I could choose to try to have sex with women. I probably could do it, but it would not feel natural to me and would not be right to her. I can choose whom I have sex with, but I cannot choose whom I am attracted to. I cannot choose who makes those tingly feelings work inside of me. That is the difference. And what most people don't understand is that the majority of what I feel being gay is an *emotional attraction* to men, not just a physical one.

This whole time that I was exploring my young gay life, I had not given up on religion. I actually reconnected with Jenny, my best childhood friend. She was involved in a Bible study group, so I joined. They were a little different from the Germany group, mostly because they were much younger. But we were all becoming pretty good friends, and I hung out with them a lot for about a year. Ironically, as I was becoming more comfortable telling people I was gay, I was also putting myself back into the closet with this group. I was creating two lives for myself, a skill that would serve me well when I rejoined the army.

Outside of the Bible study group I started to embrace the college atmosphere and spend more time on the OSU Oval. Students went out there to study, play Frisbee, hang out. It was also frequented by religious hatemongers. They were not as bad as those wicked Westboro Baptist Church people, but one day a guy stood there yelling, throwing condoms, and calling people whores and sluts. Then he started saying all this crazy stuff about gay people. I got angry, and since I was pretty well versed in scripture, I got into a crazy argument with him. Later I realized that several people from my Bible study group were on the sidelines, watching the exchange. After it was over, a few of them came up to me and said, "Hey, Steve. What has been going on with you?" I think I had yelled at the hatemonger that I was gay, so the jig was up. They pretty much stopped calling me after that.

This public outburst at the Oval likely primed me for what happened a few months later, while I was reading a letter to the editor in OSU's student newspaper, the *Lantern*. This was shortly after a big march on Washington for gay people, which several people from Columbus had attended. Someone named Dan H. wrote something like this:

"I would love to thank all gay people for going to the March on Washington because for the first time, I didn't have to look over my back constantly worrying someone was going to molest me. I didn't have to worry I was going to get AIDS. So thank you all for leaving Columbus."

It went on and on, and it infuriated me. Looking back, this foreshadowed what happened on September 22, 2011, but on a much smaller scale. For the most part I was in the closet. My closest friends and family knew about me—and now my Bible group did too—but all my classmates, professors, and everyone else thought I was straight. I knew that if I wrote a letter to the editor, I'd have to use my name. I was terrified that if I came out publicly, the G.I. Bill funds I was receiving from the army for college might get revoked. But I was so pissed that I wrote the letter anyway. This is what I wrote:

Dan, I want to let you know I did not go to the march. And if you were worried about me behind your back, don't—because I don't have AIDS, and I don't want to have sex with you. As a matter of fact, you wouldn't know me from anyone else. If you saw me standing beside you, trust me, you would not know I am gay. I am no different from you, Dan. You know what? I guess I am a little different. I served my country. I fought a war. The reason I did that was so people like you could have the freedom to write those hateful, nasty things you wrote. Yes, Dan, a *gay* person fought for your right to live in a free country and say anything you want. Have you done that?

I mailed it in. Then I rushed nervously to check the paper every day to see if it had been published. I knew I'd have to deal with the fallout, but there was nothing that could have stopped me from doing what was *right*. I think Dan H. needed to hear that he was exercising a freedom that was *earned* for him by a person whom he hated. This would be my driving force twenty years later too.

My letter did get published. I about died. A couple of people saw the article and asked me about it. That was one of my first public declarations that I was gay, and I know now that it helped me mature. I had no idea I was growing as an activist or a fighter for my rights. It just seemed like the right thing to do. Shortly thereafter another person began writing nasty stuff about gay people in the *Lantern*. I can't remember his name, but he was about to face his homophobia head on.

As I was becoming more comfortable with my gay life, I sought out movies about gay people. Someone introduced me to the movie *Torch Song Trilogy*. I will be honest; it took me a while to warm up to drag queens. They freaked me out at first. But this movie was such a great story, centered around a drag queen's life. It had a powerful message about coming out. Harvey Fierstein (the writer and star of the movie) was speaking at OSU, so I went to see him with my videotape in hand, hoping that he would sign it. (I still have that autographed tape today.)

Harvey was great, so funny and heartwarming. The audience was laughing hysterically. Then he pulled out a *Lantern* and read the hateful article this kid had written about him. I guess the LGBT group had invited the kid to see Harvey, because after reading the letter, Harvey asked the kid to come up to the stage. At first he stayed silent in the crowd. Then people cheered for him to come up, and reluctantly he did. Harvey was a powerful, strong personality. This kid was a weak, hateful bigot. Harvey raked him over the coals and embarrassed him, but then he did something cool. He gave him compassion for his hate, blamed it on ignorance. Rather than just tearing him apart, Harvey tried to show this kid support, to show him that it's okay not to hate people. He taught me a lesson about compassion that night.

I was able to spend some time with Harvey after the show and ask him about *Torch Song Trilogy*. He was such a nice man. I'm sure not every actor in Hollywood is so down to earth. Years later I also met Jim Nabors at a bar in Columbus. I still have his Gomer Pyle autograph on a cocktail napkin. I laugh when I think of how many older folks who hate gay people listened to the gospel music he sang.

Besides *Torch Song Trilogy* another one of my first influential gay movies was *Maurice*. I thought it was pretty groundbreaking because it portrayed gay people who actually loved; it wasn't all about sex. Hugh Grant's character in the movie decides he doesn't like being gay, so he leads his life as a heterosexual. Ultimately, the man he denied he loved falls in love with another man and ends up happy. But Hugh's character is stuck in a straight relationship that he hates. The woman he is with thinks she is doing something wrong because he doesn't want to have sex with her. This was the first time I realized there could be consequences if you chose to live your life in the closet and tried to be someone you are not.

Shortly after I saw *Maurice*, some friends invited me to a cookout at the home of a guy and girl who were engaged to be married. Later I found out that right before the wedding the guy told his fiancée, "I just can't do this." He explained that he was gay, and then she told him she was a lesbian. They had been dating for a while (and of course didn't have a sexual relationship), but they were both in the closet and used each other for cover. You just cannot believe the extent to which people will go to hide who they are.

My first big step in introducing my mom to my gay life was to share *Torch Song Trilogy* and *Maurice* with her. We watched both of them together, and even though I never asked her opinion, I remember it was a big deal for me to share them.

I mentioned that my parents have grown into my greatest strength. Of course the progress has been gradual but steady. My mom's support and sound advice early on really helped me see different perspectives and learn valuable lessons, particularly in handling my growing anger toward homophobia.

My mom's wisdom was about to be put to the test. One day I was with several friends and the guy I was dating at a place in Columbus called the Coffee Table. I was in a horrible mood because my boyfriend and I were having an argument about something. We were walking, and I heard this guy yelling "faggots" at us. So many times this had happened, and I had turned the other cheek or acted like I didn't hear. But on this day I was so angry and had so much rage that I yelled back at him. Then I went right over and got in his face. I had never fought back before.

"Who the hell are you to judge me?" I said.

He was a little drunk and started to take off his shirt (I guess this was a sign he was about to fight me). I wouldn't throw the first punch, but I didn't back down. So he clocked me square in the face. It unleashed all those years of rage. I beat the shit out of him. I couldn't control myself; I couldn't stop. He didn't have a chance. He was down on the ground, and I was still punching him. Later I realized how stupid that was. If I had hit him in the spine, I could have killed him.

So I ended up with a nice black eye, but he ended up much worse. I went home and called my mom and told her what had happened. She said something that was really wise but stung.

"Well, I am sure now he *really* respects gay people," she said.

"At least he will think twice before he opens his mouth," I replied.

That next day Cedar Point amusement park in Ohio had a "gay day." I went with my black eye, and you wouldn't believe how differently people acted toward me because of it. It was a mark that showed I wouldn't take anyone's shit, that I was someone who would fight back. Something else happened that day too. I wore a shirt that showed two guys hugging, and a park employee asked me to turn it inside out. The irony of that moment is that it was a "gay day" at the park. I started to question whether the park's motivation was to give people a day they could be themselves and enjoy the park or whether it was really just a day to make additional income from gay people. Little things like that constantly reminded me I was living in a bubble. I don't think that would happen today, so it seems like America's tolerance has improved.

7 Back in the Saddle, Back in the Closet

I finished graduate school in 2000 and got my first full-time job as a dietitian at a medical weight loss facility. It was an exciting time, but I started thinking a lot about the military. I had been officially out for four years. I missed it and wondered what options I would have if I wanted to go back in. I met with a recruiter and learned that with my degree I would go back into the army as an officer. So in March of 2001 an officer came to my workplace and swore me into the army reserves as a dietitian 65C. I completed all of my paperwork and was assigned to a unit in Blacklick, Ohio, where I would drill one weekend a month and two weeks a year.

The last time I'd served in the military, I hadn't even come to terms with my sexuality, so of course that was the one thing on my mind this time around. I knew it was going to be rough, but I had no idea how hard it would eventually become. I had been proudly driving around with my little rainbow sticker on my bumper, but now came the time to get rid of it. Just before my first drill I picked and picked at that sticker, but it refused to come off. I guess it was symbolic of how hard it would be to put myself back into the closet.

On a crystal-clear morning, the 11th of September, I was at work and heard that a plane had hit one of the towers of the World Trade Center. I couldn't remember which building in New York City that was. I thought it was probably a small building and had no idea that day would change not only my life but America. I called my roommate, who was freaking out and told me that there had been a hit from a second plane. Since I didn't have access to a television, I thought he was overreacting, but then came reports of planes being hijacked, terrorism, and bomb threats even in Columbus. We shut down the clinic early because no one was coming in for appointments.

When I went to drill that month, I noticed that new barriers had been set up around the facility. The war was on, and we started training as such. When I was active duty, back in the 1980s and early '90s, reservists were considered "back-fillers." The military deployed active duty troops, and reservists back-filled their positions in the United States. But as this war continued with no end in sight, it took a toll on the military's total resources. Reservists now had a greater chance of being deployed. Every time we met at drill, they would say, "You are all going to go to war again."

For ten years I walked on eggshells just waiting for this to happen. When deciding to start a relationship, I always had the thought in the back of my mind: Will this relationship last if I get deployed? Life goes on though, and you can't stop moving forward in fear of something that may never happen. The first time our unit came up on the rotation for deployment, we were not the primary unit, so we were picked apart—one person here, another person there.

In 2003 the place I worked for went out of business, and I was having a rough time getting another job. The economy hadn't crashed yet, but employers were discriminating against soldiers, even though they were not supposed to. I interviewed well and had a master's degree with great grades, but we were at war, and I was a reservist. People usually view military service honorably, but not in the midst of Operation Iraqi Freedom. Eventually I was hired as a dietitian supervisor by Columbus Public Health, where I still work today. I owe a lot to the City of Columbus; I was hired at a time when it was not very desirable to hire soldiers.

In 2005 we did our annual training (now called extended combat training) in Egypt, where it is customary for men to walk around holding hands. I was thirty-five years old at this point, but listening to the comments about the handholding made me feel like I was still in high school listening to bullies. At least in high school you could tell someone you were being bullied and get protection. In my case, if someone confirmed the bullying, then MPs would come to escort me out. Right before we had left for Egypt, a female in my unit spotted me at a gay bar. That was the first time I discovered someone else in my unit was gay. I hadn't known her for long, but it felt so good to know I wasn't completely alone. We never talked about it again after that night, but it remained a silent, unspoken comfort. It was strange because even though I knew she was gay, I still worried about someone knowing. It was that pinhole in my airtight lie.

In March 2006 I was promoted to captain and enrolled in the army's "Captain Career" course, which took place in San Antonio, Texas. "Don't Ask, Don't Tell" was in full effect, and gay people were getting kicked out left and right. Although the military had implemented the policy as a steppingstone to allow gay people to serve, it was misused to increase the number of gay people being discharged—all during a time when our nation needed these personnel the most.

My training in San Antonio was pretty standard, until we got to the dreaded "Homosexual Conduct" briefing. It was the first time I had ever heard the military's full stance on gay people. The basic premise was that the military no longer asked if you were gay, but you could be investigated if a good authority gave credible information that you were gay. Per the training, I could not self-identify as gay. I could not have sex with other men, and I could not attempt to marry another man. Those were the primary rules, but the way the training talked about gay people left me depressed and disgusted. It made me feel dirty. I still hate the word *homosexual* because of it.

Then they explained rules of conduct for soldiers who, like me, had traveled to the training from out of town. They permitted us to go out on our "off time" but warned of things to avoid, including a list of bars that were banned. Of course later I found out a lot of those were gay bars. Technically, under DADT you couldn't get into trouble for going to a gay bar. Straight people go to gay bars. It didn't mean you were having gay sex and didn't mean you were trying to marry. Yet without explanation the military gave us a directive not to go to those types of bars. It may have been to prevent fights too; I am not sure.

I started thinking back to when I had first enlisted, when that MEPS doctor asked me during the physical if I "take it up the butt." Pre-DADT you lied to the military one time, and that was that. Life wasn't necessarily easier, but it seemed completely unspoken because everyone assumed you were not gay. They were not searching for gay people or for ways to kick them out. But under DADT the possibility that there could be gays in the military was planted into people's consciousness, and with that came suspicion. But gay people under the new rules couldn't tell anyone, so that was where DADT became a witch hunt, as I would come to find out. People investigated my personal life daily with questions like, "What are you doing this weekend?" "Do you have a girlfriend?" and "What is your wife's name?" Sure, it was easy to be paranoid, but it was obvious I'd have to go back in the closet. I just didn't know how deep I'd have to go.

I was supposed to meet up with a friend who lived in San Antonio in the evening during training, but now I was nervous to hang out with him. I also wigged out a little during the training because one of the guys I met there kept using my computer, and one time I accidentally left my email open. I felt like a criminal, worried he'd discover an "I love you" note from my boyfriend. How was it possible something like this could get you investigated and kicked out? This started several new habits, like never having screensaver pictures of me and my boyfriend together, saying *they* instead of *he* or *she*, and taking pictures with my female friends so I could flash them when people asked to see my girlfriend or wife. It was a horrible way to live. I had come such a long way in my life, from hiding to slowly accepting myself but learning to hide from other people.

My phone was the riskiest part of it all. I was the tech person, so people always wanted to borrow my phone to make a call or surf the Internet. I could never put pictures of me with my boyfriend on it, and I had to install special software to try to lock out personal things. Once someone even went through my music on the phone and made antigay comments about my song library. I had to say, "Oh, my girlfriend and I dump all of our music into the same folder."

Another time on annual training I was sitting on a bus next to a military friend when my phone rang. I pulled out my phone, and the picture of the caller showed my boyfriend. My friend caught a glimpse of the phone and said, "What is that, your boyfriend?" Of course he was kidding, but imagine how paranoid I felt. I answered the call and had to be weirdly careful about what I said. The real fun happens when your partner says, "I love you." You can't say "me too" because that seems like an odd way to end a conversation. So I would say, "Okay, see you," and hope it didn't piss off my boyfriend on the other end. Josh and I came up with something pretty cool (or, rather, sad) to handle this. More about that later.

Usually I'd send out a "not safe" text to my boyfriend and friends right before someone asked to use my phone. But one time a buddy borrowed my iPhone during training to play video games, and I forgot to engage the "not safe" barrier. I sat there nervously waiting for a text that could lose me my job and my retirement. Keep in mind that these were not dirty texts, nothing obscene. None of this had anything to do with me not being able to perform my job in the military. Every time I returned home from our annual two-week training, I surrounded myself with gay-friendly people as much as possible because I had just been released from two weeks of hell trying to avoid these little traps.

People might think that if it's only the army reserves, it's only one weekend a month and two weeks a year you have to live like that. I can tell you that even one day is too much to live feeling so humiliated and demeaned. I would hear the word *faggot* more times than I could count. Showering with these people was the worst because inevitably you heard some comment like, "Hey, you faggot, I bet you want me to drop the soap." Such comments are jokes, but they really fucking hurt. I wanted to know why the hell so many people were *so obsessed* with gay people. It was crazy, like some insecurity that was out of control. And it's much more than that. I had to stay in the closet at my workplace because I always feared that a disgruntled employee could call the military and tell them I was gay or hold that over me. Nowhere did I feel safe.

I mentioned earlier that my best friend and college roommate, John, had decided to enlist in the army after 9/11. We were in the same unit, so he was the only one who knew about my sexuality. One day we were all sitting in a room, and a bunch of people started talking about the women in the unit they wanted to "bang." It was commonplace talk, but I always hated it. I hated that I had to act like I agreed. If anyone had said, "You guys are being inappropriate," people would have quipped, "What, are you gay?" John was a real gentleman. He wouldn't say nasty things about women like the other guys. I yelled at him one time when we were alone: "John, come on, man, you're gonna give me away. Can you butch it up a bit?" I was half kidding, but I was worried people would suspect me because he wasn't participating in the macho talk. I always had to balance silence with agreeing to avoid raising suspicion.

After all the years of self-loathing I started to accept and eventually embrace myself. I am a good person and have never hurt anyone else, so I began to have pride in myself. And with that I could feel my fire intensifying. So in 2006, when my friend Aaron wanted to interview me because he was writing an article about gay soldiers for a gay newspaper, I agreed. It was probably the first time fear of losing my retirement was overridden by courage to tell my story. I even let the paper put my face in the article. I knew the risk. Helping people understand the bullshit we had to go through was more important. I also thought it was a relatively safe choice because the paper didn't have a huge circulation, and if someone read it, they were probably gay too. Aaron asked me about the military's "Don't Ask, Don't Tell" policy and what it was like for me as a gay soldier. I told him: "The 'Don't Ask' part is what's not working. I couldn't tell you how many times I am 'asked' every day, but not 'asked officially.' People ask, 'Isn't she hot?' That's 'asking' me. I don't flaunt anything, but I have to dodge that every single day. . . . With all the people's homophobia, I don't know if you did tell people you were gay how it would work in the military."

Aaron also asked me about my proudest moment as a soldier, and I told him the story of how I had inspired awe in a kid I met in Sam's Club, just because I was in my uniform. I sat and talked to him, and it was obvious that the kid considered me a hero. I'm always proud when people come up to me and say, "Thank you for what you do." Still, I wonder what they would say if they knew I was gay, if they would have the same reaction.

The thing that always bothered me is that the military acknowledged we were here, serving right next to straight people. We just had to lie about it, and somehow that made everything okay. Can you imagine if we applied that logic elsewhere? If you were a murderer or rapist, for example, as long as you lied, then everyone could deal with working beside you? Of course I am not comparing a gay person to a murderer or rapist. I'm just saying that if you hate the behavior, telling someone to lie about it does not change it.

One year a guy in my unit asked if I wanted to go with him and his family to our Fourth of July celebration—"Red, White, and Boom." In my typical DADT fashion I lied and told him I appreciated the offer but was declining because I hated crowds. The truth was that I already planned to go with my childhood friend Jenny, my boyfriend, and another friend. I went to the event, and at the point in the evening when they honored our military, you could see the patriotism on everyone's faces. Looking up at the beautiful fireworks blasting in the sky, the percussion that ricocheted in my chest was as deep as the pride upwelling from my heart. I got chills and felt so appreciated . . . for about two seconds.

Then I had an epiphany, and reality set in. The speaker announced that we owed our freedom to the men and women in uniform, all while I was cowering so I wouldn't be seen with my boyfriend. I was this noble, honorable patriot, and I was protecting everyone's freedom—except my own. Each firework that exploded from that moment on unleashed a firestorm of tears that turned to anger, then rage. Walking back after the show, I ranted to my friends about how living in a "free country" was such bullshit. "This freedom means having to lie to protect it for everyone *except me*, the one fighting for it," I shouted.

Just as I was being *very* vocal about it, someone kicked the back of my leg. It was the guy who had invited me to come to the fireworks. I instantly tried to alienate my boyfriend and my other friend. I clung to Jenny and introduced her. I was awake all night worrying that he had heard my diatribe. The worst part is that this guy was my friend, someone who had asked me to be the officer to perform his reenlistment oath. And I viewed him as a potential enemy if he heard or saw too much.

Being closeted in the military not only made things more difficult for me but also prevented me from doing my job in the most effective way possible. Later a really nice, quiet kid transferred into our unit, but I noticed a couple of times when he came in for drill that he had marks on his arms. It turned out he was cutting himself. I talked to him extensively to see if I could help. I was on numerous conference calls about him, but as a reservist I had a much harder time getting things done because I saw everyone only once a month. After a couple more months of drill and more cuts on his arms I pushed again to get him help. My command listened and said I should take him to Fort Knox for an evaluation to see if he was in danger of harming himself and whether he was fit to stay in the military. Before we went, they gave me his files to pass along to the military, and in them he had disclosed he was bisexual. I wanted so badly to give him some guidance or advice, and I thought it would be better received from me, someone to whom he could relate. But I couldn't tell him I was gay.

I tried to offer as much support as possible during our four-hour drive to his psych evaluation. I wouldn't tell him I was gay, but I told him he should be honest in his evaluation and that the army had his best interests in mind. I cautioned him to not focus on talking about being bisexual. I said I would try to support him, tell them that he did a good job, and vouch for his character. But if he mentioned the bisexuality, that would be it. It was buried in that file, so I hoped that maybe they wouldn't notice or say anything about it. As a civilian I could have offered him support. But as an army captain doing so would have meant risking my entire military career. I had never been so frustrated in trying to help someone.

After his evaluation the military decided to process him out. He was so upset he nearly cried. I don't know the real reason for his discharge, but I hope it was because of the cutting issue more than his bisexuality. I will never know. On our return trip I gave him as much compassion as I could without self-revealing. When we got back, I spoke with his mom to try to provide resources for him. I didn't want to just cut him loose. He was a good kid. He just needed help.

He was allowed to come to a couple of drills until they processed him out, right before "Family Day." I loathed Family Day. Most gay people I've talked to since the repeal of DADT are on the same sheet of music. Being forced to honor other people's spouses and families without being able to talk about our own is a slap in the face. I would put on a smile and meet everyone's wives and children while making up excuses for why my girlfriend couldn't come. Being there alone, with no family, gets harder and harder to justify as you age. When people like Rick Santorum say I want special privileges as a gay person in the military, I would like them to experience this.

This particular Family Day coincided with that kid's last drill. He had nothing to lose, so he brought his boyfriend. To this day I'm amazed at the balls this kid had to do what he did. I was horrified, but curious to see the other soldiers' reactions. Based on the antigay comments I heard all the time in my unit, I knew they would not be accepting. But what I observed was an interesting dynamic. All around me I heard *fag* and all sorts of derogatory comments. But the commenters were all cowards: none of them said a word to his face. They just mumbled in the company of people who they thought agreed with them. That taught me a huge lesson about courage.

That kid will probably never know it, but he inspired me to one day be as courageous as he was. This was my first chance to see the reaction my unit would have toward a real, live gay person. And I was surprised. Homophobic people are cowards.

8 This Looks Like a Gay Dude's House

The guys in my unit constantly asked about my fictitious girl-friend. They wanted to know if she was hot, how old she was, what she looked like, where she worked, if we were going to get married. At one time I used a picture of an Asian friend of mine who was kissing me while I was playing pool. They even made up a nickname for her, "Miso" (appearantly for "me so horny"). My boyfriend had his own place but stayed with me almost all of the time. One evening my boyfriend and I were in the privacy of my own home, sleeping. My phone rang in the middle of the night. Three of my army buddies were drunk and wanted to stop by to play my arcade game, which I had built from scratch. I told them I didn't think it was a good idea, but they insisted.

They said, "We're on our way," and then hung up. I panicked. I woke up my boyfriend and asked him to leave. Like we were in a fire drill, we both jumped up out of bed. He quickly got dressed, and I ran around the house hiding pictures of us. I was forced to clean my own house in the middle of the night, thanks to DADT. I felt so bad for my boyfriend. How dirty would it make you feel to be told to leave in the middle of the night? He was a trooper, didn't even flinch, and went fast so we wouldn't get caught. This practice of hiding stuff was not uncommon, and I had gotten quite proficient at it.

Right before he got ready to kiss me goodbye and tell me he would see me later, my drunk soldier friends called me again.

They said they had changed their minds and wouldn't be coming over. That made the whole thing even worse.

"You guys are going to get your asses kicked," I threatened.

"What, did we piss off Miso? Is she mad?" said the snarky voice on the phone.

My boyfriend heard the whole conversation. When I hung up, he said, "It's best if I just go to my house." So I went upstairs and cried about the whole situation. I never felt like a bigger piece of shit than I did that night for disrespecting him and living my life like this.

I really hated my life. I hated living like I was in prison. It was hurting my relationship. And it was all so fucking stupid. Was this a "special privilege"? Was this about sex? I was not asking to have sex in the military. If given the chance of a rebuttal after Mr. Santorum answered my question with his "sex has no place in the military" and "gay people want special privileges" rhetoric, I would have told him that story.

In addition to the drunken drive-by that almost happened, I've had several other close calls in the DADT witch hunt. Over the years I had become good friends with a guy in my unit named Troy. While John was deployed, Troy and I palled around together a lot. I always thought that if I would ever come out to anyone in the military, it would be Troy. Then he asked me something that made me rethink this. We were on our way to annual training, and I noticed that the flight attendant on the plane was wearing a rainbow bracelet. Troy asked, "Do you know what that bracelet means?" I wondered if this was his way of asking about me, but he seemed a little uneasy, so I just played dumb.

All of my friends, including my boyfriend, played video games at my house on the weekend. It was a total nerd fest—we'd stay up all night and order pizza. This was my "gay life." Troy always asked if he could join, and I really wanted him to, but I couldn't risk it. I didn't know how he would react. So

I always made up excuses for why he couldn't come over. He asked me again one day, and I decided to test the water.

"I want you to, but there is something I never told you about my roommates," I said.

"What?" he asked, seeming a little cautious.

"Well, they are kind of progressive."

"What do you mean, progressive?" he said nervously.

This was my invitation for him to say, "I don't care," or "I'm cool with whatever." But he didn't. So I slipped into lie mode.

"They smoke pot," I said, to which he answered, "Oh, I don't care if they do that."

This was a failed attempt. In truth my roommates did not smoke pot, and one of them was later offended that I had made him sound like a pothead. Plus I really wasn't thinking what my roommates must have thought of me being so willing to throw them under the bus to test the water to see if he would accept them (when it was really about me). So I went back into the safe closet from Troy. We went through a couple more years of me dodging the issue and putting necessary limitations on our friendship. Toward the end of his military service I slowly tried to hint a little more and even invited him to my house a couple times. Of course I hid some pictures and other obvious pieces of evidence. One day Troy stopped by while I was in the middle of my workout, so he went upstairs to play with my computer until I finished. At that very moment my boyfriend came over without my knowledge and went upstairs to put away our laundry, so it was pretty obvious. But Troy never said anything. But he also never acted different toward me.

During our last Family Day, when Troy was almost finished with his military service, I started talking to him about having gay friends. He didn't seem freaked out. So I blurted out, "Do you know about me?" He smiled and said, "For a while now." He told me that every time he came home from drill, his wife asked, "Did Steve come out to you yet?" Then he said, "I wish you would have said something because I really wanted to play video games with you guys!" For the first time I realized that I had wasted years of a great friendship in hiding. To this day Troy and I are good friends. Part of my decision to come out to my friend Renshaw in Iraq in 2011 was directly the result of wasting years of a friendship with Troy.

The last couple of months in the military with Troy were fun because together we secretly laughed at all the homophobic comments. He told me about a bunch of unattractive and overweight soldiers who were talking about "queers" wanting them. Troy had no qualms about walking up to them and saying, "No queer would ever want any of you guys. Don't flatter yourselves."

Just as Troy was preparing for the end of his military career, I met another friend, Matt, on extended combat training. He was as much of a tech geek as I am, so we became fast friends. I talked him into transferring to our unit, which meant he'd have to drive much farther to the battle assembly, but he agreed. Then it became apparent that he thought we could hang out on the weekends, so I had to dodge that bullet. He was also someone who always asked to see pictures of my girlfriend.

One time drill ended too late for Matt to find lodging, so I offered to let him stay at my place for the weekend. So I did a quick run-through at my house. My roommate was out of town, and I asked my boyfriend to stay at his own house. So Matt came over and dropped off his stuff. The first thing he said when he walked through the door was, "Dude, this looks like a gay dude's house!" I about shit. First of all, my house wasn't that abnormal. The guy I was dating loved to decorate, so he had made the house look nice. He had painted all the rooms and hung a few pictures and plants, but it wasn't effeminate. I didn't know how to respond, so in defense I said, "How do you know what a gay dude's house looks like?" It's funny how quickly you can defend yourself. But even my defense was a bit homophobic because I was accusing him of being gay.

That comment made me weirdly standoffish toward Matt. We played video games for a while, then decided to work on our iPhones. I went to bed wondering whether this stuff was all in my head. I look back to Troy and know I wasted all that time that I could have had a good friendship. If you never give someone a chance to show that they can be cool, then you always stay a little shy and weird and secret. But there is so much to lose all the time. My life was like the show *Dexter*—not because I was a serial killer but because my whole life was a lie. Everything out of my mouth was always carefully thought out. Even now I sometimes have a hard time remembering not to call my husband *she* just because I got used to that. My friend Renshaw in Iraq was the first person to make that *Dexter* comparison once he found out.

Once again it was embarrassing and demeaning to tell my boyfriend he wasn't welcome in my home the night that Matt stayed over, though asking him to leave in the middle of the night that one time was definitely worse. And when I called him *she* on the phone, I always thought that hurt his feelings. That takes a toll on relationships, and I think it's one of the things that contributed to our breakup. It sucked, but it's just one story out of thousands of troops who've had to live their lives like this. And many of them still do. Just because the army says we don't have to lie anymore doesn't mean it's easier to tell people. We still have a mindset and culture to change before we will know it really doesn't matter to people.

A case in point is the comment I got from a fellow soldier's girlfriend.

"Where do you live?" she asked.

"Columbus," I replied.

"Ewww! How do you live there?" was her response. "There are way too many gay people. I couldn't stand that."

I have dealt with so many of those shitty comments in my life. The odd thing about this hate is that people don't know they are being directly hateful to another human being. I always wished we had a stamp that said "GAY" on our foreheads. That way there would be no coming out to anyone. People could avoid you if they had a problem with you. I used to come home and say that one of the these days I was going to take one comment wrong and burst out right in front of formation and tell everyone I was gay! I would let them deal with the shock and think about everything that came out of their mouths from then on. Of course that was just a fantasy. I never thought it would actually happen. The best thing about coming out to everyone at once during the debates is that, even though it made me vulnerable, it also caused the people who hated me to just stay away. It's the nicest shield I could have had.

On the Internet people can hide behind their hate. Just read the comments on YouTube or on people's Facebook posts. Are the commenters meaner than they really would be in person, just because they can post anonymously? Are they revealing their true selves? There were so many comments online in response to my appearance at the 2011 debates. One person wrote: "I hope that queer gets AIDS and dies." I often wonder if he would say that to me face to face. I doubt it. But it is amazing that he found it acceptable to say it on the Internet, hiding like a baby. Even worse are the fake people. They treat you one way, but behind your back they are different. Those people make me sick, so I choose to exclude them from my life as best I can.

9 ~~Jessica~~ Josh

Even though I'd had a couple of long-term (four years or more) relationships since coming out, I consider my story up to now the story of my journey alone. It wasn't until I met Josh that I knew my journey would never be alone again. Before I met Josh, I was longing to find my true love. I used to go to gay bars and just feel miserable. I would watch people and want something other than a party or a one-night stand. Often I would sit back in a corner and watch people, get a little depressed, and go home. One night I really hit bottom about not having found a life companion, but I remembered the thing that had helped me process my thoughts and emotions during my first tour in Iraq—my journal. So for the first time in years I sat down and wrote in a journal. Here's an excerpt:

> To be alone is such a bitter feeling. I often wonder how people can do it. When I go out, I don't know how to display my emotions so a stranger can look right through me into my heart. The *only* person in the entire world who knows the true me is me. So if I keep the intimate details of myself on paper, one day someone else might have the opportunity to know the real me too.
>
> I ache for so many of my friends who will never experience the love that I have in my family. My family is so wonderful and has taken in some of my less-fortunate friends as brothers and sisters. I want so badly to one day have a family of my

own with my soul mate. I really wonder if that's possible. I know you are out there. I know you think about me too. I am so hungry for compassion, not sex. I fall asleep every night and hug my pillows so tight pretending it's you. I don't have any idea what you look like. I don't care. How do I know what to say to you when I see you? How will I know it is you? I am so lonely waiting for you that I want to be extremely careful not to be blinded by someone pretending to be you.

Nothing in the entire world could make me feel how I feel when I play the piano. I am so fortunate to be able to play. I don't know how I can; it seems almost genetic. It's a gift I feel my dad has given to me. What a joy to know that every time I strike a key, my dad is there playing with me. This makes me want so badly to have children. The piano has been my salvation for as long as I can remember. This diary is not unlike that. It feels so nice to type whatever comes to mind and not worry that it will be judged, ridiculed, mocked. I have so many emotions bottled up inside and so many things I want to share with the person who is out there for me, so I have to start sharing them with something. And it feels good to share them with this diary. I don't really know what the purpose of this is. I just know deep in my heart that it needs to be done.

A friend of mine invited me to go out for a night of karaoke, and reluctantly I decided to go. Josh also happened to be there that night. My first impression of him was that he was beautiful. He was tall and had a smile that was so bright and captivating it could stop traffic. It's not surprising that his smile was the first thing I saw because he smiles a lot. I didn't talk to him; he was with a group of people, and I just wasn't in the mood to interrupt. I had a roommate at the time who was friends with Josh and would talk about him to me, but I never knew it was the same person I had seen at karaoke until much later. Josh's friend used to talk to him about me, too, and later I found out from Josh that we both thought the other person sounded cool. It was by chance that Josh came over to my house looking for my roommate, and I met him. It was weird that I knew of him, but all the connections, all the many things we had in common, started to make sense. I'm not sure how we had missed meeting each other, as often as he and my roommate Adam hung out and played video games.

Since I was a little kid I have always loved video games. I owe that to my grandfather. When I was little, my brother and I would go with my grandpa to the American Legion, and he would give us quarters to play games together. He was the person who introduced me to an escape from the darkness that plagued my childhood. When I buried him, I put a quarter in his hand, cried, and walked away. So my passion for video-games started in childhood but continued into adulthood. As an adult I built a full-sized arcade machine that plays thousands of games. I jokingly call it my four-hundred-pound child. When Josh came over, we instantly connected, and I marched him upstairs, proud to show him the arcade. I could tell right away that either Josh was really genuinely interested in the machine, or he was excited to see how enthusiastic I was about it. He kept on smiling the whole time I demonstrated it to him. I could tell that his inner nerd had started to see how much we had in common. We were both geeks; we both loved technology; we were both witty and smartasses all in the same package. We instantly connected as friends destined to be something more.

As our friendship intensified, so did the time we spent together. The initiation of a relationship came during lunch in Columbus with some friends. There had been lots of flirting and talking up to that point, but he went out on a limb at lunch and broke the tension by grabbing my hand and holding it. I didn't resist. If he had been anyone else, I probably would have never spoken to him again, after I punched him in the face. But Josh and I have always had this nonverbal communication I cannot explain. It's like we understand each other's thoughts, and I'm sure that when he reached out for my hand that day, he knew I would be okay with it. I am not one to kiss and tell, but our first kiss was truly magical. I have never in my life been so attracted to someone, not only physically but emotionally.

Josh then asked me to come to Chicago with him to help a friend move. I really wanted to go because it was my chance to spend a couple days with him and decide if we should take this to the next level. There was almost no notice, and I am usually the type of person who likes to plan everything out, but I went. In many ways Josh started to add to my personality and complete me as a person. Things that I would not spontaneously do, I wanted to do with him.

We truly fell in love during the six-hour car ride to Chicago in June of 2010. Not only was Josh someone to whom I was deeply attracted, but he was also quickly becoming my best friend. While we were in Chicago, we went to take a nap. We were lying next to each other for a while, his head on my stomach, just talking about our families. He shared details about his personal life that he'd never shared with other people, and he remarked how weird it was that he felt so comfortable with me. There is never judgment between us; we accept each other, flaws and all. We had the best time during that trip, and I didn't want it to end. The drive back seemed like it was over way too fast. The closer we got to Columbus, the more anxiety I felt that this moment was about to end.

After Josh dropped me off at my house in Columbus, I watched his car pull away and immediately felt empty. It was a feeling I hadn't had since the day my mom dropped me off at kindergarten for the first time. I knew then that I was falling deeply in love with him. So many uncanny coincidences happened at just the right time to prove we were meant to be together. It was like no force in the universe could have kept us apart or kept us from meeting. Eventually we would have found each other. Now I know that only when you find true love do you know what it is. I had said the words before to other people, but I never truly meant them until I said them to Josh.

As we grew closer, I knew that inevitably DADT would impact our relationship, as it had always done in the past. One of the particularly terrifying times happened at the Ohio State Fair. Josh's parents build these cool, artistically crafted wooden rockers. Early on in our relationship Josh and I were helping his parents display their rockers at the fair. We were sitting in the booth, close enough to hold hands, smiling at each other. I reached out to covertly hold his hand, and I looked up to see one of the guys from my unit with his wife, holding hands. I quickly ripped my hand away from Josh's. Josh looked at me, really confused; I was initiating him into my life of lies and secrecy. But despite the usual stress on relationships posed by DADT, Josh and I continued to date and fall more and more deeply in love. One thing I feel with Josh that I never felt in the past is that he really is my best friend. No matter what, I want him to be with me. We could go to a Laundromat and have the time of our lives. Nothing was not fun, as long as Josh was at my side. I have heard of people falling in love, realizing they were meant for each other and getting married quickly, but I never thought I'd be one of those people.

One of our first confrontations with what we were about to face under DADT was the constant barrage of people asking me about my girlfriend. For many years I would just say I didn't have one. But then I started to fear that this would cause suspicion, because when someone is perpetually asking, red flags start to go up in curious minds. So one time my roommate jokingly called Josh "Jessica" because we had to hide who he was all the time. Unfortunately, my roommate was also a victim of the game of lies under DADT. I remember a time when one of my army buddies came over to my house unexpectedly, and my roommate and his boyfriend were there, having accidentally locked themselves out of the house. My army buddy called and said some stranger was trying to get into my house. This caused me all kinds of grief at the time. But the alternate identity "Jessica" started to stick. It was perfect. I asked one of my lesbian friends, Joanna, if I could take pictures with her and use them for cover. Sadly, I was now prepared for the next time someone caught me with a question. I was slowly learning how to become a professional liar: You can't have inconsistencies in your story. You can't mess up and use a different name or a different picture.

We got notification in June that our unit was deploying, but rather than the entire unit, it would be only the sections they needed. For the past ten years I had lived under the constant threat that there was a chance I would be deployed. I had become numb to it. My reality was that, in my previous relationships, a deployment would not have been threatening. But now I had found my life partner, and I was terrified that deployment could ruin what I had waited for my whole life, especially this early in the relationship. The moment came when I was told they were taking my section and I had a one-in-three chance of being the dietitian deployed. Then I was told we were not going, so I was pretty convinced I was in the clear. Josh and I were in the process of deciding to move in together. I had just taken a promotion at work, and everything was at its peak.

What people don't realize about military spouses is that there is constant stress about deployment. Even though I was told I was safe for the time being, I lived in a constant state of readiness to give up my life on command. That causes so much tension and uncertainty in developing relationships. Many relationships cannot endure a deployment, and the army works hard to help ease that burden. But lots of relationships can't even endure the tension of the possibility of a deployment.

Then one day at work my cell phone rang. It was our unit administrator. It was weird that he was calling me, since he'd only call if he needed a document signed or something like that. Normally I would never take cell phone calls at work, but this time I answered.

"Sir, I am calling to tell you that you are being deployed with the unit," he said.

My blood stopped flowing, and my stomach turned. "Are you serious?" I replied. "I thought they already left for Kuwait."

The people in my unit who had been deployed had left a couple of months ago for premobilization training, so this news was shocking. He said he was 100 percent positive, so I made a couple of calls to command to confirm and find out what was going on since being picked out after the premobilization process had started was so abnormal. I was being pulled late, so late, in fact, that they were figuring out how I would catch up to my unit in premobilization training. My life flashed before my eyes. Mostly I was thinking that for the first time in my life I had found true happiness and companionship. I don't think Josh ever really thought this could happen. I knew that pulling my hand away from Josh at the fair had started to introduce him to my army life, but the reality of going to war was an entirely different story. I could handle being deployed. What I could not handle was if his reaction to this news was, "I can't wait for you." That's what I was trying to prepare myself for. And that thought was definitely more frightening than the thought of going to war or even dying at that point.

I came home for lunch, and Josh was upstairs, on a conference call. I looked very somber. Josh and I communicate extremely well without words, so he could tell something was wrong. He put the call on mute.

"What is it?" he asked.

"It's bad," I said.

He looked scared and really couldn't focus on the call, so he hung up and sat down to talk to me. I told him I had gotten the call, that I was being deployed. Those words stuck to the roof of my mouth like peanut butter. I will never forget the empty look in his eyes. For a second he looked like me, full of disbelief (I think his brain was trying to process my words), but then he held me.

"I understand if you don't want to wait for me," I told him.

"Are you kidding me? I will be right here for you," he said.

I thought to myself, this man is too good to be true. All the lack of commitment I had experienced in past relationships had made me vulnerable and fearful that I might lose Josh over this. This was a big step; he would be putting his life on hold with me, not to mention that he'd have the responsibility of taking care of all my stuff while I was gone. It was like I was dumping a full-time job onto him: paying my bills, taking care of my house and dog, being there if I needed anything across the miles. I looked him in the eyes, and I said, "If you wait for me to return to you, then I will marry you. You are the one for me." He said, "I will wait for you." We held each other and cried.

They didn't give me much time to prepare. I had to tell my employer that I was being deployed. I was on a quick flight to my SRP (Soldier Readiness Processing). At this point there was no talk about the repeal of DADT (or at least I didn't know about it). Legal told me that I had to designate a power of attorney. The army is very strongly against soldiers designating a full power of attorney, especially to a "friend," which is exactly what I did. It was a very awkward moment. I had to tell them that this friend was trustworthy, and I had to be counseled about my liability. Again I was about to be shipped off to war and an unknown future, and I was sitting there worrying if this person was suspicious of my relationship with Josh.

I also had to change my life insurance and will. I listed Josh under the category of "friend," but I wondered what would happen if I got killed. Would he be the last one to know? When I got back from the SRP, I had to sit my family and Josh down and tell them my wishes if I were killed. Josh later told me that this conversation was very uncomfortable. We really hadn't dated a long time at that point. We were close to each other's parents, but that is an awkward conversation to have at any time with any parents. But I knew he was "the one," so that pushed us ahead. One of my biggest fears came from hearing so many stories of gay people who had lost a partner whose family turned on them as the surviving partner. There was nothing in the law that would protect Josh if my parents didn't honor my wishes. I was lucky because I knew my parents would never do that. Many people are not so lucky; some are even denied the right to attend their partner's funeral. So it was very important for me, with such an unknowable future ahead, to have this uncomfortable conversation.

Time flew quickly, and November 6, 2010, came before I knew it. The day I left, I remember feeling fine, like I was going on a trip. But I took one last glance at my dog Macho and started thinking about how he didn't understand what was going on or why I would disappear from his life for a whole year. That made me sad: I hugged him and started bawling. Most of the Columbus soldiers being deployed met at the unit to take a bus together, but I got special permission to drive to Cleveland and leave from there so I could spend more time with my parents and my "brother." Josh, my parents, and I met Josh's parents for lunch in Cleveland before the report time. After lunch Josh and my parents waited in the car while I checked in. I saw people hugging and kissing loved ones goodbye and thought to myself, I am so glad the van's windows are tinted.

We drove the van across the street from the unit, behind some construction vehicles for cover. My parents gave Josh and me time to say goodbye. My dad is a marine. He served in Vietnam. He is proud of me and proud of my military service, yet he had to park that van behind some vehicles like we were criminals hiding in shame. Like we were second-class citizens.

Again the fire inside of me was turning into rage, but right now it was muffled by sadness.

I kissed Josh goodbye, not knowing that I would actually get to see him a couple more times before leaving the United States. I looked back at my parents in the van as we hid our kisses; the whole situation made me feel so low. I went into the unit and watched my loved ones drive away. I was alone.

Our unit is split into thirds geographically, so a lot of the people around me were strangers, strangers who would have to become my family for an entire year. A family I had to lie to. My reality before had been so different. Once you come out and get comfortable and secure in yourself, being asked to go back into the closet is devastating. But instead of presenting a once-a-month, two-weeks-a-year challenge, DADT would now be affecting me twenty-four hours a day, 365 days a year, every second of my life. This is such an additional stress on a soldier. There was no escape, no one to turn to. I was leaving behind everyone I loved, everyone who knew the real me. I started to question myself, wondering whether I'd be able to handle it.

Toward the end of our predeployment preparations in Cleveland the unit held a yellow ribbon ceremony, inviting our families to proudly see us off to war. This was something I usually felt excluded from, but it was my last chance to see my family. I really wanted Josh to come too, so I figured I'd just tell people he was my brother. It sounded easy on paper, but once I saw him, it was a struggle not to hug him. I spent the whole time worried that people would wonder who Josh was. It was like I was being mean to him, rejecting him, but I couldn't help it. We began marching into the venue, and I saw Josh staring at me. He had a tear in his eye. He later told me that was one of the hardest things he'd ever had to do, to sit there emotionless trying to watch while pretending he was not my lover.

The next morning we went off to Seattle, where we would endure a month of pretty rigorous premob training. Josh's birthday was approaching, and I hated that I had to miss it. People take for granted how much soldiers give up—the birth of a child, a child's first steps, birthdays, deaths. I ordered a basket of flowers and treats to be delivered on his birthday. I talked with him on the phone as much as I could while I was in Seattle, until I overheard another soldier in the bay where I lived talking to his wife on his cell phone. I couldn't believe how easy it was to hear whether the voice on the line was male or female. That freaked me out. I made sure from that point on to lower the volume on my phone to a point where I could barely hear so when people heard me say, "I love you," they didn't know I was saying it to a man on the other end.

The cover of "Jessica" was not enough. I needed to be careful because "Josh" came up on my phone for his calls and texts. Texting became much safer, hiding that I was gay. The only thing I had to watch was that I never let someone borrow my phone. So Josh and I had safety measures. "Hey are you busy?" meant, is it safe, or, is this you? We all learned such basic survival skills under DADT. One time I typed, "I love you," but the iPhone auto-corrected it to "Oliver." So it became a joke that we would say "Oliver" instead of "I love you," but it really was a useful code word, so sad. I often wonder if Rick Santorum ever had to do that.

Thanksgiving was coming, and we were given a four-day pass before we headed out of country. Josh and I decided that even though it was expensive, he would fly to Seattle, and we would get a hotel for those four days. It was our first Thanksgiving together as a couple. It had been less than a month since I last saw him, but it felt like eternity. Funny how time goes fast when you don't want it to and slow when you do. Like when you were a kid and you thought it would be a lifetime until the school year ended. Then summer came, and life was great, and then it was all over in three seconds.

Of course the whole time with Josh I was worried I might bump into someone else on a pass. Just to be sure, I started telling people that my brother was in town on business, and I was going to visit with him. We had so much fun together in the city. We went into an antique store, and Josh showed me a Bible he had seen on a previous trip that was hundreds of years old. I knew we wouldn't have Christmas together, so I kept thinking how cool it would be for him to receive a gift from me that we saw together in Seattle. I made arrangements to buy the Bible for him and have it delivered on Christmas. Little did I know that we would eventually be married in front of that Bible.

After a wonderful Thanksgiving together we ate one last meal and headed to the airport a few hours before my bus came. I bumped into another soldier in my unit, so I introduced Josh as my brother. The soldiers were all starting to congregate out in the common area with their spouses. Josh and I tried to find a place where we could talk and play Worms, a video game we loved playing together. We found a safe haven underneath an escalator. We played, but the game was anything but fun. We tried to pretend we weren't going through all of this and that everything was normal, but I knew my pending doom was near. I was getting emotional. So was Josh. I peeked out from our hiding place and saw all the wives hugging each other and meeting one another. I saw them exchanging phone numbers for support. I looked over at Josh, and he was all alone. There was no one there for him to talk to; he had to try to keep dry eyes and put on a facade of being my brother seeing me off. It was time to go, and we both instantly started crying. We checked to make sure the coast was clear and then headed off in different directions like perfect strangers. That was the hardest thing I've ever had to do. This was really goodbye, for a long time. Maybe forever.

10 Cemetery Ceremony and Insensitive Sensitivity

After the horrific plane ride I described at the beginning of this book, life actually got a little easier when we arrived in Iraq. I had anxiety getting off the plane. I remember being curious about the smell of the air. My mind took me back to Desert Storm, and I kept wondering if I was really up for this. Being an officer, I had more privacy than I did during my first tour twenty years earlier. I got into my routine with my mission there and was able to start working out, which has always been a great stress reliever for me. I also met Renshaw, a soldier from Michigan. He asked me if I could help him work out, so he became my workout partner, and as our friendship grew over the year, he became my best buddy in Iraq.

The approach of the winter holidays was particularly hard. There was no snow, no Christmas spirit. Sure, chow hall was decorated, but it felt more like a movie set designed to create a contained, limited reality. A lot of us felt like we would have been better off without the decorations; they reminded us too much of what we were really missing. Thank God for Skype. I never had anything like it when I was in Desert Storm, and it made my second war so much easier. I was able to watch my parents and my nieces open their gifts. I was able to see Josh open up his Bible and could tell from his expression that he realized how much planning I had had to do to make that happen. My mixed bag of emotions included the extreme happiness of being part of Christmas in some way, along with the emptiness of being away from them all and feeling excluded. I tried to mask my sadness over Skype. When I clicked "end call," it took me back to Desert Storm and hanging up the phone and how hard that was.

When you are in Iraq, you don't take anything for granted—your friends, family, a flushing toilet, Christmas, work, weekends. You miss it all so much. And time does not pass quickly. Then I made the connection, again thinking back to summertime in grade school, that life passes us quickly when we take things for granted. We never know what tomorrow will bring—a car accident or a heart attack can drastically change your world. I vowed right then to make the next Christmas with my family last forever. I would make the next time Josh and I took Macho on a walk seem like an eternity.

A couple of times when I was Skyping with Josh, all of a sudden there would be a huge explosion. The military trains you on what to do if you are being attacked with mortars: you grab your gear and go to a bunker. So systematically, I would say, "That's a mortar, I have to go," clicking "end call" without giving Josh a chance to respond. Then silence. We both often wondered whether, if something happened to me, Josh would even find out. It wasn't until years later that Josh shared his perception of those mortars, but more about that later.

I received a handwritten letter one day during mail call—*handwritten*. It was from Josh's mom. She could have sent an email in three seconds. It wasn't the words that mattered most. The whole process—having to get out the paper, the pen, address the envelope, put a stamp on it, and take it to the post office just to say, "Hi, I am thinking about you"—really made me think. I have a DVR at home so I can skip through commercials. Don't let your life be like that DVR; don't skip through things that add depth and quality to your life.

The holidays passed, and I started to read some things in the newspaper about the repeal of "Don't Ask, Don't Tell." Being gay, you get used to disappointment. Every time you think you score a legal victory for gay people, something like Proposition 8 in California gets passed. I have never understood the drive people have to discriminate against gay people. If they can't stop us from marrying, then by God they will stop everyone from saying *gay* in school. Insane. In the back of my mind I was sure DADT wasn't going away. It had been so much a part of my reality for such a significant period of my life that it didn't seem possible that it could be gone.

At the end of April, halfway through deployment, I went home for fifteen days on R&R. Little did I know this would change my life. The flight home was so much more exciting than the flight over to Iraq. I got to the Columbus airport and had a flashback of my homecoming from Desert Storm in 1991. I was much older now, but I still had butterflies in my stomach to see everyone. It felt like an eternity since I had seen them. I dropped my bags and ran and squeezed Josh so tight, it's a wonder I didn't hurt him.

My R&R went quickly. There were so many people to visit, and so many things I wanted to do, it gobbled up my time. Josh and I had a blast, as usual, and time flew. One night, we were out to dinner in Columbus, knowing our time was coming to an end, and it reminded us how much we wanted to be married someday.

"I would marry you right now if I could," I said.

"So would I," he said.

At first it sounded like we were playing a game of wishful thinking, but then our voices started to change inflection as we talked about possibilities. "Don't Ask, Don't Tell" was still in effect, but I had read in the paper that the army was no longer enforcing it. So was this my green light? I had to think hard of the implications and consequences of our actions. My desire to marry Josh overwhelmed my fear that it could threaten my retirement and military career.

Finally I said, "Why don't we do it now, while I am on leave? I don't leave until Friday. What if something happened to me?" We talked about those mortars. I told him, "What if one of them had hit me, or what if you were in a car accident? I don't want to think that if I died I would have never been married to you."

I knew that this man was the one. He was giving up a year of his life to wait for me. Any relationship that can make it through a deployment can make it through anything! We started looking into it, but I only had three days left of my R&R. Gay marriage at the time was legal in only a handful of places in the United States, and one of them is Washington DC, the birthplace of all the laws that discriminate against us. We discovered that there was a three-day waiting period to get a marriage certificate in DC, but when we called to ask about the wait time being waived, we were told it was possible if we had a good enough excuse (and that being deployed to Iraq was a pretty good excuse).

We hung up the phone, and for a moment my stomach sank.

"Did you tell them we were gay, and it's two men getting married, when you asked about being on leave from Iraq?" I said nervously.

I didn't know if that made a difference, but living a life of discrimination for so long made me worry about it. We called back, and thankfully the woman on the other line laughed and said it didn't matter. That felt good.

We got into the car on May 3, 2011, and headed for DC, a six-hour car ride that was as much fun as our first six-hour drive together. And just like before we fell more in love along the way. We laughed so hard at one point that I couldn't catch my breath. I had so much fun with this man and knew marrying him was the right decision. Once we arrived in DC, it was chaos trying to make everything happen. We were hungry, and the only place we could find to eat was called Lola's, which was also the name of the restaurant where we had eaten our Thanksgiving dinner in Seattle before I was deployed. This was yet another funny coincidence that to us was a sign of the inevitable.

We wanted to find a civil officiant in DC who specialized in same-sex marriages, and that led us to Tiffany Newman. She was very warm when we spoke on the phone, and she offered several sites for the ceremony. We told her we wanted something significant. I was a soldier home from Iraq, marrying the man of my dreams in a district that had just started to recognize gay marriage. She recommended going to the Congressional Cemetery because that was where we could find the grave of Leonard Matlovich, a Vietnam tech sergeant and veteran whose headstone reads, "When I was in the military they gave me a medal for killing two men and a discharge for loving one." We weren't sure what kind of omen it would be to get married in a cemetery, but the choice seemed meaningful.

We did some research on Matlovich and learned that he had been discharged from the air force in 1975 before the military had any formal policies about being gay. He fought back against his dismissal and actually won. Since he was a decorated servicemember, the military couldn't prove why he should be discharged. He settled the case for $160,000 (what his retirement would have been) due to worries that he would be treated badly if he went back into service. He was a pioneer who probably helped to pave the way for the DADT repeal or at least drew attention to gay rights in the military. As one of the most famous gay rights activist at the time, next to Harvey Milk, he was featured on magazines and talk shows, noting similarities between his story and the way African Americans were treated and trying to bring his fight for equal rights to the world at large.

We found Matlovich's grave and were stunned by the headstones all around it: Gay World War II Soldier, Gay Vietnam Vet, Gay Businessman, Gay Schoolteacher. There was the (gay) son of the founder of the Boy Scouts. Some plots had been purchased and were awaiting future use. Seeing this unknown section of the cemetery was profound. A guy walking his dog nearby asked if we wanted to know the significance of this site. He told us that J. Edgar Hoover was buried here, and so was his lover. (He lived in the closet.) That explained why so many people wanted to be buried here. I looked around, and sure enough, I saw both gravestones, though that of Hoover's lover was down a ways because he couldn't be buried close to Hoover. That was even more of a reason to get married here. This was a way to honor the happiness that had been denied all of these people.

When Matlovich was alive, marriage between two men was not a possibility. Now a soldier still on active duty and currently deployed in Iraq was able to come home on leave and marry his partner for two reasons: the repeal of DADT had just been approved, and DC had legalized same-sex marriage the previous year. That is everything Matlovich fought for: what a way to honor his legacy. It was the close of his story and the beginning of ours. It was perfect. People always envision their perfect wedding with cakes, meals, family, and all the details just right, but that day was all I wanted.

So on May 3, 2011, Josh and I were married. This day was far more wonderful than the most expensive wedding ever. We decided we'd have another ceremony later for family, but this was just about us. Josh's mom said we had to have something borrowed, something blue, something old, and something new. Our borrowed was a little bride figure that belonged to our roommate Adam. Our blue was the tag from our dog Macho's collar. Our old was the antique Bible I had bought Josh for Christmas; it sat on Matlovich's tombstone while we performed the ceremony. Our new was an iPad that I had just given Josh as a gift while on R&R, since we are both technophiles who love to geek out and play computer games together like Worms, Angry Birds, and chess. It's amazing that so much thought was put into something that was executed so quickly.

The Royal Wedding had nothing on us. Later we were offered the opportunity to purchase the plot beside Leonard's grave. We did. We will proudly be buried there together.

Did I mention that I had received literature from the military earlier that week that warned us to not do anything different until the repeal of DADT became final? Oops! It reminded me of a condescending comic about the DADT rules called *Dignity and Respect*—how ironic. The comic stated that you couldn't tell anyone you were gay, engage in any homosexual act, or try to marry someone of the same sex. I had just done at least a couple of those things. How perfect was it that our excuse to expedite the wedding was my deployment to Iraq? Everyone in DC was so nice, and they seemed proud of us. Even the judge who approved the time waiver said, "We wish you both the best."

We exchanged rings and drove back to Columbus as a married couple (until we crossed the Ohio state line). Two days later my leave came to an end. Sometimes I think leave makes army life more difficult. You get a little teaser with your family and loved ones for fifteen days, and then you have to head back to hell. Sitting at the Atlanta airport on my way back to Iraq, I got a voicemail from Josh. He was shaking and crying, telling me how much he loved me and how hard all this was. Then he said, "This has been the most amazing two weeks of my life, this is so hard, and I love you." I sat there in the airport bawling like a baby. To this day I have that voicemail saved, and I'll never delete it. I still listen to it.

My ring was my commitment of love to Josh, and I wasn't taking it off for anyone. When I returned to Iraq, people immediately asked me about it. I didn't want to move it to a different finger, and I was getting tired of lying, so I decided to tell them I had gotten married, not realizing the hole of lies I'd have to dig. I hardly ever talked about dating out of self-preservation, so this was a surprise for people. Right away they wanted details. Sure, I could have taken it off, but I was done with that shit. I tried to be as true to the story as possible but just changed the sex of my spouse. Where I really started to slip was when people kept telling me I needed to visit S-1 (personnel) and apply for my benefits as a married person, which include family separation and increased housing allowances. They were genuinely interested in making sure I got my benefits, but that put me in a place where I was really getting pressured to tell the truth. So once again this shows that DADT didn't work. If I wanted to quietly wear my ring of commitment, I was not permitted to do so.

One thing that infuriates me is that under DADT people were getting booted out of the military left and right. But due to our extended involvement in the Middle East, the number of discharges started decreasing. People who got discovered were told to go to war and warned that the gay issue would be dealt with when they returned. In other words, in a time of need the U.S. military has no problem sending gay people to combat. They send us because we are good soldiers, because they know we do a good job. The fact that they process us out of the military when we return from war shows that this policy has nothing to do with ability to serve and everything to do with hate and discrimination.

The questions about my ring just kept pushing me to feel like eventually I'd be forced to tell the truth. It was all coming to a head. This was also about the time the Republican presidential candidates, including Michele Bachmann, started showcasing their antigay platforms. Then our company commander went on R&R, and the guys in my unit painted his door pink and added flowers and all kinds of feminine flourishes to it. The rest of that prank played out during an awards ceremony a few weeks later, when the recipients skipped up to the front, saluted in a stereotypically gay manner, and started slurring and lisping their speech. Everyone was doing it, including people in command who should have known better. Talk about a hostile workplace. To this day I don't think any of them have thought about how badly that hurt my feelings, but they didn't have to have awareness; they were protected. I kept thinking about how interesting this would be once the repeal went through, which finally had been assigned the date of September 20, 2011.

The next thing that added fuel to my twenty-year-burning fire was SHARPS (Sexual Assault and Prevention) training, which is supposed to teach military members how to identify and prevent sexual harassment and discrimination. This is an attempt to cleanse the military of rape against female soldiers. Rape and assault are a real problem in the military, especially during deployments, and this again underscores the irony of Mr. Santorum's claim that sex has no place in the military. While the trainer was giving out the EO (Equal Opportunity) phone numbers where you could report harassment, he stated, "If you commit an act against a female soldier, you will go to jail. And when you are in jail, Bubba will take care of you when you drop the soap. So don't do it."

So in an attempt to prevent harassment, this trainer perpetuated a stereotype against gay people and condoned rape against a male as punishment for harassing a female. I was so pissed, but it wasn't time yet. I didn't have protection to stand up for myself, so I set up an anonymous email account and sent a complaint to the EO office. Here is an excerpt of what I wrote:

Hello Ma'am,

I am writing this from an anonymous email for obvious identification reasons. I want to complain that <name removed to protect identity>, who just did a training on POSH/Sexual Harassment & Assault/Equal Opportunity for our unit, used offensive non-EEO-friendly language. He repeatedly referred to punishment for violating someone sexually as going to jail, where "Bubba" will bend you over and rape you or where you will get a "boyfriend." With the repeal of DADT, I would hope that the first people who receive sensitivity training are the POSH/EEO trainers, so they don't say ignorant comments like this. This comment personifies a stereotype that gay people will rape you. If I had made a comment about Hispanic people being lazy and not wanting to work, then I am sure I would have offended <name removed>. Well, same thing. I would never rape someone. Neither would any of the gay people I know. So, please let him know this is offensive and should not be tolerated. It is evident to me that if I can hear this rude, offensive language in an Army sensitivity training, then we have a *long* way to go.

Thank you,

Anonymous Soldier

Of course I never received a response, not even an acknowledgment that the complaint had been received.

Shortly after that I attended a new type of training session—one that had been created in response to the repeal of DADT. The official September 20 repeal date was still a few months away, but the military had to start preparing us for the change. I felt awkward, mostly because this training was about me, even though at that point I didn't intend to ever tell the military I was gay (even after the repeal). People attending the training seemed very serious and somber, quite a different vibe from the lisping and name calling that were rampant not too long ago.

Based on my bad experiences with EO training in the past, I wasn't expecting much, but I was surprised. The instructor showed a short video and went through some scenarios. Of course a couple of people in the group said some inappropriate things. One person wanted to know how gays could be allowed in when sodomy was still illegal. Someone told him that it was not illegal. I was surprised that someone would say anything that could be perceived as defending gay people. Then another soldier complained that since two guys are allowed in a CHU

(Containerized Housing Unit), but males and females are forbidden to share one, gay people were being permitted to do something heterosexual people couldn't do, and that was discrimination. Though his point was valid, I took exception to the equal-treatment argument. I wondered if he had ever had to run around and hide pictures of his wife. But males and females were forbidden to share the same CHU as a rape-prevention measure. There would be the same expectation of gay people in terms of conduct. Sexual intercourse was forbidden. Again people couldn't abandon the thought that if two men who might be gay were living in the same quarters, certainly they would have sex. Again my mind goes back to Rick Santorum: I asked about being allowed to serve in the military, and he took this to mean having sex in the military. Then the first sergeant, who was part of the training, said something cool: "Look, people, the army is changing, and if you can't change with it, then it is time for you to get out." I liked that statement. It was strong. Other points of the training seemed a little unfair. For example, if someone is hateful toward a gay soldier, the victim is not protected under Equal Opportunity and instead has to go through the chain of command (which can be uncomfortable). But the Inspector General channel is available if the chain is part of the complaint.

I also didn't care for the statement that being gay "is a private and personal matter" because when people show me pictures of their kids or wife, they are not told that their family is a "private and personal matter." It was like this was an "it's still better if we don't know, so keep it to yourself" option. A lot of the training also focused on reminding me what benefits Josh and I would *not* be entitled to, such as housing allowances, family separation, yellow ribbon ceremonies, "Strong Bonds" counseling, and on and on. They were so clear on what gay people could not receive that it seemed like they knew how unfair this was and were anticipating a potential backlash of people asking for equal treatment. This was a lot of what ended up motivating me to ask the second part of my question (which never made the cut) to the Republican candidates. It makes you angry when people tell you that your relationship is not as significant as everyone else's. It was just as hard for me to be separated from Josh as it was for anyone else, gay or straight. Still, the training was far more respectful than the army's only other "homosexual briefing" I'd had to endure, in my earlier years.

I don't know why, but during this training I felt a little like a zoo animal that people were learning how to feed and pet. Overall the training was good, and the awkwardness was mine, but the whole thing reinforced my intention to never come out to anyone. I remember posting to my friends on Facebook that just because I was allowed to be in the military didn't mean people were going to change their culture or their prejudice of gay people.

11 The Debate

Since you've read the first chapter in this book, you know that my resolution to stay closeted to the military came crumbling down the minute I uploaded my video to Google. But for about an hour before that fateful click I just stared at my laptop, watching my life flash before my eyes. I went through every moment of being pissed off by the things people had said over the years. I started remembering all the times I'd had to alter my life to make everyone else feel comfortable, all the freedoms I'd had to give up over and above what straight soldiers sacrifice to serve their country.

With each memory my blood pressure rose, and my fists clenched harder and harder. The final straw was hearing a group of candidates, most of whom had never served a day of their life in the military, threaten to take everything away and force me to go through it all again. So I hit send. Fuck them, I hit send. That simple click of the mouse set off a shockwave that "outed" me to the world and placed me in the unusual predicament of being booed on national television. Then adding insult to injury was Rick Santorum's horrible answer to my question. Here is the transcript:

RICK SANTORUM: I would say any type of sexual activity has absolutely no place in the military. And the fact they're making a point to include it as a provision within the military that we are going to recognize a group of people and give them a special privilege too, and removing Don't Ask, Don't Tell, I think tries to inject social policy into the military. And the military's job is to do one thing, and that is to defend our country.

MEGYN KELLY: What would you do with soldiers like Stephen Hill?

SANTORUM: What we are doing is playing social experimentation with our military right now. And that's tragic. I would just say that going forward we would reinstitute that policy if Rick Santorum was president. That policy would be reinstituted, and as far as people who are in, I would not throw them out because that would be unfair to them because of the policy of this administration. But we would move forward in conformity with what was happening in the past, which was, sex is not an issue. It should not be an issue. Leave it alone. Keep it to yourself, whether you are heterosexual or homosexual.

I don't know where to begin. I know this has been analyzed to death, so I will just give my perspective. Right now rape of female soldiers is a huge problem in military deployments. So if you want to take the ignorant stance that sex has no presence in the military, then females will continue to be raped. I never asked Mr. Santorum (or anyone else) if I could have sex while I was doing my military job, but I think he knew that. He was trying to manipulate his answer so people would be confused and think that gay people are asking for special permission to change military conduct. Gay people have never asked for that. It is quite the opposite: I don't want to be different or to be *treated differently*. I want the same standards as everyone else. I want to live under the same code of conduct as every other soldier.

The next part, which I love, is "they are asking for a provision to get special privileges." I would like to know if Mr. Santorum has pictures of his wife and children inside his home. And I would like to know if he lives in constant fear that he will lose his job and benefits if someone happens to come into his house and see those pictures. If that is a special privilege, then I must not understand the extent of how much he despises gay people and gay soldiers. I want to know if he has to turn the volume down on his cell phone so people cannot hear that he has a wife, or if he has to claim his wife is his sister and hide her under an escalator to say goodbye.

Santorum did say one thing right: the military's job is to defend our country. We do that job and do it well. And we have been doing it with gay soldiers—lots of gay soldiers—for a long time. Under DADT the military discharged more than fourteen thousand soldiers just for being gay. And the vast majority of those discharges had nothing to do with conduct, just with whom those people chose to love. Unless you have ever worried that you may have left an email up and the sender's name could be signed with "Love," you will never understand what it is like to live in constant fear of being found out.

And when Megyn Kelly asked Mr. Santorum what he would do with me, it was clear that he hadn't really put any forethought into his statements: he had backed himself into a corner. He was probably thinking, "I just told a soldier currently serving his nation in a warzone that I'd reinstate a policy that would kick him out." Awkward—as I sat there blinking at him from the monitor. Then his answer changed to, "As far as people who are in, I would not throw them out." Tell me, Commander-in-Chief, how do you write a policy for that one? New homosexuals could be discharged, but those grandfathered in would be safe? Would I still have to hide my pictures in my house? Would I still have to call Josh my wife? He just threw up his hands like a kid who can't formulate a logical conclusion. And somehow he was a candidate for president of the United States.

When I go back and watch the debates again, I wonder if Megyn Kelly tried to help Santorum avoid botching up the answer. She introduced my question as, "This question raised a whole lot of controversy online." Ding ding! (Please be careful with your answer, this is going to be a controversial question.) Then she said, "It comes from Stephen Hill, a soldier currently serving in Iraq." Ding ding ding! (This is a soldier; please watch it because people love soldiers.) Then the "currently serving in Iraq" should have been a key to say, if you tell this guy you want to reinstate the ban, you are basically telling him that you don't think he can do his job.

The last thing he said was, "Going forward, we would go back to Don't Ask, Don't Tell; sex has no place in the military. Keep it to yourself, whether you are homosexual or heterosexual." I must say that I would *love, love, love* if we could do this, because it's the only way people could understand what gay people have been through all these years. What a sensitivity experiment for straight people. I would love it if no one could talk about their families. I would love it if I didn't have to look at naked women on people's cell phones. I would love it if I didn't have to respond to interrogations about my girlfriend. I can't imagine not hearing a soldier complain about a fight he and his wife had the night before or another saying that he and his wife were going to a movie tonight. What would happen if a straight soldier's parents were the only ones who could be notified if he or she were killed in war because his or her spouse wasn't recognized by the military? Heterosexual people would go insane. They wouldn't last a week. We've done it for our whole lives.

Now let's talk about the booing. I've read so many responses about the booing, everything from, "It was only a few people," to, "It was a Democrat planted at the debate." Someone even said I wasn't a real soldier, that I just dressed up like one and sent in the question. People have even accused me of having asked a "gotcha question" or said that the question was very inappropriate. I was in the middle of my second war in twenty years as a soldier who had to hide pictures in his own house to serve his country. A stage full of political leaders, most of whom had never served in the military, threatened to take my right to do that away. That question was not a "gotcha"; it was my reality. It was more than a couple of people who booed me that night. It was the entire auditorium. I say this because when Rick Santorum said he would fight to prevent me from being able to serve openly, the whole audience cheered and clapped. So when people say that the audience booed the question and not me, the gay soldier, my response is to ask them about the standing ovation that came at the notion of kicking me out while I was over in Iraq and they all sat in Orlando, Florida.

After I listened to his answer, I turned off the television. There was total silence. I had just come out as being gay to every military person, my high school friends, my teachers, my coworkers, and all my relatives, as well as everyone else in the world. There was no taking that back. How was I going to face all these people I was deployed with? My first thought was maybe they hadn't seen it.

Josh and I Skyped and talked about the whole thing. He was very excited that the question was out there. I was so nervous about the fallout. Then he said, "Oh my God. Google 'booed soldier.'" That's when I started to realize the scope of this. Instantly, outraged people were blogging, and then the news started reporting the incident, and then all the comments . . . I was in trouble.

So I went to my friend Tims. She knew I was going to ask the question, but we hadn't known if it would air. I told her I was a little freaked out and didn't know what to do.

"I'm going to tell you what you're gonna do," she said. "You are going to walk over to chow and hold your head up high, shoulders back, and be proud of yourself."

I did as she suggested but tried to avoid talking to anyone because at this point I didn't know who knew and who didn't. I was suspicious of everyone. The airtight lie that had protected me for twenty years had been blown open with a hand grenade.

Because of the time difference Josh was asleep as it was all blowing up, but it was the start of my day. I was trying to see what was happening, frantically thinking about how to keep a handle on things. I didn't know if I should go tell my commander. At one point I Googled the word *gay*, and I was five of the top hits. I was horrified by how huge this had gotten so fast; it was not what I intended. I really needed Josh, but he was asleep.

I went to lunch with Renshaw. We were at the salad bar, and all of a sudden I looked up at the twelve big monitors in our giant chow hall, which holds over a thousand people. All of the TVs were showing the news, and I was on every one of them. My life was on display. I knew by asking that question, I would be coming out in a big way; I just had no idea it would keep going on and on. A couple of days later at the gym I was on all the TVs again. Every time this happened, I just looked away, trying to act like I wasn't hearing it, but I knew people were pointing and whispering. I felt humiliated.

The day after the debate I had a meeting at the army hospital where I worked. This would be my first face-to-face confrontation with multiple people in my unit since the debate. Renshaw told me that everyone was running around with laptops showing each other the YouTube clip of my video. When I walked through the ER, a soldier grabbed my arm. He looked at me, and it was a real surprise to hear from him so directly.

"So are you signing a lot of autographs?" he said with a reluctant smile, not knowing how I would react.

"Yeah, I know a lot of people are shocked because I wasn't out to anyone," I replied. "This is pretty awkward."

He looked puzzled, then grabbed my hand and rubbed it on top of his hand. "Why is it awkward?" he said. "Your gay is not going to rub off on me."

I was dumbfounded. I didn't expect that, not from him especially or anyone else for that matter. He went on to tell me that his brother had married his partner a couple of years ago. He and I had never been close here in Iraq, but having that common bond seemed to make us respect each other a little more. Later I asked if the *Brokeback Mountain* comment during our plane ride over here had offended him. He answered, "Yes, it pissed me off." That restored to me the confidence this exposure had taken away. My suspicion was confirmed: there were straight people with gay relatives and friends who were equally hurt by those antigay comments.

I knew how it felt to come out of the closet; I had come out years ago to my family. But I had forgotten how liberating it feels not to have to lie to people. Now I didn't have to make up a fake name for Josh when I said something about him feeding the dogs. You can't imagine how nice that felt. This entire time, by my door in my room, I had kept a chewed-up toy and an empty poop bag from Macho, to remind me of him. I had a love note from Josh that he had only signed with his initials. Now for the first time I hung a picture in my room in Iraq of Josh and me holding our rings. For the first ten months in theater I had always worn headphones when Skyping with Josh so nobody could hear me talking to a guy. I didn't have to do that anymore. I was no longer afraid to put a picture of Josh and me on my computer. It was like an entire world of weight had been lifted off my shoulders.

I know not everyone in the army is cool with me being gay, but the people who aren't have lost their power. Before I was invisible in front of them. I sat there and absorbed all of their insults. Other people would go along with the negative comments and jokes because they didn't want to be labeled as gay by standing up for others. The whole tide has turned. The homophobic people are like cockroaches, running toward a dark corner. They now have to secretly find allies who think like they do. They have to keep it to themselves. They have to do all the stuff I used to have to do. For once the tables were turned. Other people started coming out of the cracks to show their support for me.

You can always tell when a person is really cool or downright homophobic. The cool ones don't run from you, and they're not afraid to ask questions and learn more. One of my soldiers came knocking on my door. He came in and sat down but looked perplexed. He asked, "Do you call him your wife?" He was very young, and it was an innocent question. He wanted to know more about it and was sincerely intrigued.

On the opposite side of that spectrum one very conservative guy sat down with me and another person at chow. We had always talked before the debates about politics: he would argue because his views veered far right, and mine did not. But after the debate came dead silence and avoidance. But then finally one day we sat next to each other in chow. We had a good discussion, and it was a chance for me to talk to him about things I thought were issues for him. He mentioned his apprehension about the showers. After my initial thought, *Please don't flatter yourself, buddy*, I told him that I probably felt more awkward in the showers than anyone else because I was paranoid people would be uncomfortable with me, and it made me really standoffish. I explained it like this: "If you think gays can't shower without separating themselves from sex, then we should also ban male gynecologists. Obviously they cannot separate themselves from sex once they see that vagina. We are professionals, and I go to the shower simply to get clean, not for a peep show and not for any other creepy thing. That notion actually freaks me out."

For the most part my experience with DADT being repealed is that nothing has changed, other than the fact that people are learning to be considerate and realizing that they cannot say harmful things without consequence. People liked and respected me before, and once they realized I was the same person they've served with all these years, it became clear to them that my sexuality really doesn't matter. One thing that has changed since the debates is that I don't have the luxury of anonymity. So now when I go to a shower, everyone knows I'm the gay dude. For the rest of the time in Tikrit I'd wake up at 3 a.m. to shower or try to go when I knew no one else would be around. If anyone asked, I'd tell them I was trying to adjust to my schedule back home. The funny thing is, this had nothing to do with self-control; it was completely a case of me trying not to make my fellow soldiers uncomfortable. Despite having to do this shit for years, for some reason it's in my nature to protect other people's comfort level before my own. Nothing makes me feel more uncomfortable than making someone else feel uncomfortable.

A lot of people don't realize that part of my attraction to men is their ability to reciprocate my attraction. I think that's the same for a lot of gay people. Sure, I can think someone is attractive, but for me to be attracted to them in the way that makes some straight people uncomfortable, they have to be gay. Throughout my military career I have never had an impure thought about another soldier in the shower. I was hoping these guys would realize that I had been showering with them for twenty years and had not hit on anyone, raped anyone, had an impure thought about anyone, or done anything except get a shower and brush my teeth.

I was talking about my "laws of attraction" to that conservative soldier who was a little homophobic at first. We then started talking about perceptions of gay people in general. I asked him, "Hey, what do you think [name omitted, an older woman in our unit] looks like naked or what she likes to do during sex?"

"Ewww, that's gross," he said.

"What kinky stuff do you think she does in her bedroom with her husband?" I asked.

Again he said how gross of a thought that was.

"Exactly," I said. "So why is it when I mention I'm not at-tracted to women, that's the first thought that goes into your head? Extend me the same courtesy that I give you every day. It would make me nauseous if I went around trying to con-template what people did when they had sex, so why do you do that to me?"

He said that made sense to him. Later he would tell me that I had made a profound impact on what he thinks about gay people. I mentioned that he is very conservative, to the point of referring to Rush Limbaugh, Sean Hannity, and Glenn Beck as the three wise men. He knew I am very liberal, that I love Rachel Maddow. Of course he despises her; she's like his kryp-tonite. Since he pummeled me during the entire deployment with Rush Limbaugh quotes, I joked with him later that if I ever met Rachel in person, I would tell her to do a shout-out to him by name, acknowledging him as her number-one fan. Little did I know that in the near future I would have that opportunity, and I would seize it.

The definition of marriage was another popular topic of con-versation with him. As he became more comfortable talking to me about this, more of these discussions kept coming up. I asked him why gay marriage bothers him so much.

"Gay people don't want to marry you; we want to marry each other," I said. "So how does that affect you in any way? If any-thing, it leaves *more* women for you!"

"Then where does it stop?" he said. "Can pedophiles get mar-ried to children? Can multiple people marry? What if someone wants three wives? Should that be legal?"

My answer to him was that if no one is getting hurt and it is consensual between adults who are old enough to understand their choice, no one should care if they marry. It isn't their busi-ness. Obviously marrying a child isn't consensual. I went on to tell him that I personally could care less if five adults want to marry; that's their prerogative, but that isn't something I would choose for myself. My philosophy is that if it doesn't directly affect my life and it's not hurting anybody, then I have no business condemning it or really having an opinion about it. I wish more people felt the same. But this whole dialogue with him would have never happened had I not come out, and I know he better understands gay people as a result. So I believe this all happened for a reason.

What I don't understand are the crazy passionate people like Rick Santorum. That guy has devoted his life to fighting gay people and their rights. Someone asked what his main platform for his presidential campaign would be, and he brought up fighting gay marriage. He has hate so ingrained into his core that he makes it the focus of his life. Often people with this much hate come out as gay themselves; their homophobia is a cover for something they never want to be discovered.

I knew I had a lot to lose by asking that question, but I never imagined the freedom it would open up for me. The most important thing I hoped that would come out of this was to expose the raw homophobia and hate among powerful politicians. People holding these offices can change doctrine and policies, so their power is a serious threat. I think my question revealed that.

12 The Fallout

I didn't have to respond to Rick Santorum. America responded. And it restored my faith in my country. Almost immediately after the debate Josh sent me links to many websites where responses kept pouring in. People were outraged, not just in America but all over the world. I was seeing my story on news stations in Britian and receiving emails from everywhere. At one point, Google emailed to ask where I wanted all this correspondence to go.

Over the next two weeks my life was under the microscope of the public eye. My most intimate secret was being talked about on every TV station in the world. *The Daily Show with Jon Stewart* had a clip that poked fun at my arm size; it reaired on CNN, MSNBC, Fox News, *Headline News*, ABC, even *Real Time with Bill Maher*. The kicker came one night at about midnight when we had a quick reaction force (QRF) drill. We were woken up in the middle of the night and had to get out to our guard post with all our gear on, a drill we did randomly in Iraq. I ran out and was guarding my post when a fellow soldier said to me, "I saw President Obama was talking about you." I don't think anyone ever thinks they will hear that in their life, but sitting in Iraq, it was my reality.

So I ran back to my room to see what he had said when he spoke at a dinner for the Human Rights Campaign. As I sat and watched, I started to tear up at his words. He condemned the candidates for not standing up for me. He said, "If you want to be the president of the United States, then you can start by standing up for our men and women in uniform even when it is not politically convenient." To this day words cannot express how wonderful it feels to have President Obama's support. I was proud to be deployed under the first African American president and especially to hear him defend me. Later I thought about his life and the things he had gone through and wondered if it was easier for him to relate to me. At one time his mother and father could not have married because of laws that prohibited them. At one time if he had served in the military, he would have been segregated. Either way that day made me very proud. Before all the chatter got any bigger than it already was, I walked into my commander's office to let her know I was the booed soldier who was all over TV. I was nervous. First, what if she judged me for being gay? Second, what if she was pissed off about what I had done? I respected her and valued her opinion of me. My voice shook as I told her. And without blinking an eye, she said, "Captain Hill, I don't care if you are gay; I would take ten of you if I could. I have no problem with what you did. I'm just glad you're not bringing me something worse than this."

I don't think she realized the enormity of the situation at the time. About thirty minutes after our discussion I received a page to come back to her office because a CCIR (Critical Incident Report) had come down from headquarters in response to what I had told her. She explained that the military's primary concern was to make sure I was protected and that no one was messing with me. I was really touched by that and thought it showed a huge mindset change for the army. Just a month ago no one had responded to my complaint of the harassment training, and now they were concerned for my well-being. It made me extremely proud to be a soldier. The military took command and made sure this was being handled professionally and without incident. The command sergeant major also visited me personally to make sure everything was okay and that no one was making any comments or harassing me.

So many people in Iraq said they couldn't believe all the controversy this caused. Lots of people told me what I had done was very brave, and I received a bunch of hugs. I got some negative reactions, but not many. Several of my soldiers told me they thought I had only said I was gay in my video because I was standing up for another gay soldier I might have known. I was known to speak out against bigoted comments about black people and women, so at first some people assumed that's what I was doing.

One of my fellow soldiers in a high-ranking position told me that a few people from our command were not excited that I had appeared in uniform in the video, as it is against army policy to be in uniform at a political event. But they did note that since we were in a theater of war, we didn't have civilian clothes. When I spoke to the military lawyers, I explained that I originally submitted the question without my identity or rank, and I made sure that I was in compliance with military protocol before doing so. They concurred that as an American I had every right to participate in the debates. A couple of them actually told me, "Good for you for standing up for what you believe in."

I received a Skype message from a friend who connected me with a young soldier stationed on the same base as I was. The kid told me, "Sir, I don't know you, but I want to thank you for what you did. I think it took an incredible amount of courage to do it. I will probably never tell anyone else in the army that I'm gay, but you stood up for us all." He went on to tell me that someone kept using the word *faggots* during their training. That made me mad. I instantly shifted into "I want to protect him" mode.

I also received an anonymous email from someone pretty high up in the Pentagon. It read, "Your younger generation has an easier time coming out than our older generation does.

I don't know if I can ever come out, but if I do, you have made it easier for people like me."

This was all hitting home with me, and it made me feel proud for standing up for so many people. Another big eye-opener came when a soldier asked if we could talk after church services that day. She told me that she hadn't been honest with me. When I asked about what, she said, "The same thing." Someone I'd known for more than ten years, both serving in silence, came out to me. Under DADT she had always asked about my family, so I had always felt paranoid around her when we talked. It blew my mind that after all these years not only was she *not* trying to invade my personal business, but she was plagued by the same policy. Because of DADT we had persecuted each other with the same kinds of questions. She has been with her partner for more than fifteen years, and anonymity has become their way of life. To this day she still has no intention of coming out.

All the while the Internet kept exploding. People mostly were very supportive, though occasionally they'd write things like, "I hope he gets AIDS and dies." Other people said army enlistments would go down because of me. The negative and hateful comments were definitely the minority, but they were still a wakeup call. Alfred Baldasaro, a New Hampshire state representative, said he was happy people had booed me and that my brothers and sisters in Iraq would now probably let me die in war. My fellow soldiers took a *lot* of offense to that comment. They would never let another soldier die, gay or straight, and it was presumptuous for him to label soldiers so narrowly. The response to his hateful comment was so great that there were calls for him to step down. Josh mentioned later that it would be interesting to publish a book of these negative comments and let them all speak for themselves.

The reality is that no one in my unit had been negatively affected by my presence. In fact I'm pretty sure most of them appreciated having me around. I did a lot to boost morale, including organizing karaoke shows, which people loved, helping people with diet and exercise, and even teaching some computer skills courses. Some of those things weren't required; they were just examples of me going above and beyond to provide some entertainment and enjoyment during our time at war. It was an extension of me always worrying about other people's welfare.

I really was the barometer for gauging the repeal of DADT, both for how "unit cohesiveness" would work, since that was the main argument against gay people in the military, and for how chaplains should and would respond to gay soldiers. People are going to come out gradually, over time, so it's hit or miss whether they encounter people who have a problem with it. I, however, came out to everyone all at once, so if there was going to be an issue, I would've encountered it. You know what? I had zero problems. If anything, what I did opened the door for better communication.

I mentioned that those hateful comments (most of which were from people not in the military) were a wakeup call that we have a lot more work to do to break down this enduring culture of bigotry. It inspired Josh to post a heartfelt comment on Facebook, so I'm including a snippet of that here:

"I've got to go, I think that was a mortar . . ."

As you sit there and ponder, evolve, or debate your stand on equal rights, think about this: You're pondering *my life*. Imagine your husband, wife, boyfriend, or girlfriend halfway across the world. You haven't seen him or her for nearly six months, and instead of your normal goodbyes, your conversation is interrupted by an explosion, and the line disconnects. That happened to me today, and it's not the first time.

Now imagine someone tells you that your love is corrupt or disgusting. Imagine thinking that if something ever went wrong, you could be the last to know, if at all. Imagine knowing that a hospital could deny you access to your loved one upon request of a family member. Imagine being left behind to manage life without any support.

The next time you're asked what your stand on equality is, put yourself in my shoes, in the shoes of the LGBT community. I have a chip on my shoulder. I have avoided and even denied it, but I can't anymore. I am married, but in the state of Ohio right now that means nothing. If Steve had been killed by that mortar today, I might not have found out for weeks, maybe even months. While I am lucky because our families would not allow that, I can't help but realize how so many are not as fortunate. I have been complacent, but I will not be anymore. If you are my friend, support equality and if you don't, my suggestion to you is keep it to yourself and stay out of my way.

This past year has opened my eyes; this past hour has filled me with passion. I will not accept being content, I will not accept separate but equal. Character is not shown in a time of comfort; character is shown in a time of challenge, and consequence. I'm going to build character, real character, are you?

As Josh said in his blog, we were hit by mortars on a couple different occasions. Those were the times when reality hit home: the military does not consider Josh my husband. What if something happened to me, and no one called to tell him? What if something were to happen to him? They would not give me emergency leave to go home and bury my husband. Those were the moments that made me ask the second part of my question at the debates—and join the Servicemembers Legal Defense Network lawsuit. More about that later.

After the repeal of DADT there was a little bit of protest from chaplains, who claimed they would have to alter their convictions and beliefs. The military responded that they didn't have to change their faith or the way they preach. This makes sense to me because there are soldiers of all faiths. Some don't believe in God. Chaplains are not only spiritual supporters; they are people with whom soldiers can discuss grievances.

The entire time in Iraq I liked our chaplain a lot. He and I had whiled away many an hour in Iraq having conversations, including about my falling out with religion in my younger years, but I had never told him I was gay. In one conversation I was brave enough to tell him that I fell away from religion because I didn't like the way religious people treated my gay brother. That alone was scary to throw out there, but I thought it could help me talk more about being gay and religion. We'd talk about my marriage (I just didn't tell him it was to a man), and he'd encourage me to attend his marriage classes because they provide insight on how to handle finances and other household issues. He suggested that we Skype with my wife. Of course I had to turn him down. You become so delusional, you actually start to believe your own web of lies. I listened to his advice and applied it to Josh, and I started to feel like it was nonbiased sincere advice, like it was all I had. But now every major news station was reporting the central fact that I had always omitted from our conversations.

Once the chaplain found out, it opened up a lot of dialogue. He invited me to lunch one day, and I broached the topic by posing this question: "How did military chaplains ever condone a rule that would cause people to sin? He looked confused, but I told him that military chaplains should have been fighting DADT all along because it forced gay soldiers to lie, and lying is a sin." He really didn't know what to say, and that wasn't the first time I had left him speechless in our conversations.

We then got into the age-old conversation of whether or not I was born gay. He believes upbringing rather than genetics is at play for gay people, and as proof he pointed to cases of identical twins where one is gay and the other is not. I have seen tons of gay twins in my life, so our perspective on that is different. Then I asked him if animals can sin. His first answer was, "No." So I said, "Many species of apes are predominately homosexual, so if animals can't sin, then is being homosexual a sin?"

I told the chaplain many of the stories included in this book, like about trekking into the field at night and praying for God to change me and going to a seminar to "pray your gay away." Open and honest conversations like these are the first step in breaking down prejudice, but it's a delicate balance. If you say too much, it's easy for someone to jump in to "save your soul" and take a position that's contentious rather than neutral and supportive. At the end of our lunchtime chat I don't think either of us had changed the other's views, but that's okay.

A few weeks later the chaplain asked me to have supper. When he came to pick me up, he was carrying a bundle wrapped in a shirt. He said it was a gift for me. He handed it over with trepidation and said, "If you want me to read anything in return, I will." That was my clue that it had something to do with being gay and that I probably wasn't going to like it.

In the shirt were four books on changing your sexuality through God. I snapped back to the seminar at OSU and what I thought of that guy. This made me realize there would be a learning curve in how chaplains interact with gay soldiers. I tried to convey to him that the only reason I didn't tear his face off (my words) when he gave me those books is that I like him and know that deep in his heart he's doing what he thinks is right. When I revealed that for much of my life I had tried to change myself, he must have mistaken this to mean I was asking for help. I told him again that if there were a pill I could take to become not gay, I would take it, solely because it's easier to live in society as a straight person. But I also let him know that there is no pill, and I am no less proud of myself for being gay. But I have learned to accept and love myself and to be proud of who I am.

Being religious and being gay don't have to conflict. There is so much harm in making people think that they can just flip a switch and change. I am here to say that for whatever reason God made me this way. I was born this way, and it's not wrong (just ask Lady Gaga!). Actually I am probably a better person as a result of everything I've had to endure in my life. It forces me to try to understand other people's perspectives. It has taken me a long time to accept this. But I am finally here. I was going to give the books back to the chaplain as a nice gesture, but instead I threw them out because they do more harm than good. I would never want some kid reading that kind of smut.

Our time in theater was finally growing short, and I started to see the light at the end of a very long tunnel. When we deployed, our unit was split among four different sites in Iraq, and each of us ran a hospital at each location. At this point we received word that the four sites were going to be consolidated in Tikrit in preparation for our move home. This was rough for me because it would be the first time in almost a year I'd see anyone from the other three sites. The people at my site had had time to acclimate and talk with me about being gay, and by the end of our time in theater it was no big deal to them. I had started to think of them as my allies. Consolidation would be like going through the awkward coming-out phase all over again (I would be faced with the same thing back home with the portion of my unit that hadn't been deployed). Videos of the debate had played so often that I think most people could recite my question. There was no lying low.

I was comfortable in Tikrit because it's where I had spent the most time, but I knew not to let my guard down yet because this would be the first true test of tolerance for people I hadn't seen for most of the year. I would have to share a tent with some of them for a couple of weeks, and I wasn't sure what to expect. People from the unit, including the other chaplain I knew, greeted us when we arrived. The other chaplain wasn't shy at all, and he joked with me about trying to watch the interview clip where Jon Stewart made fun of my big arms.

When I got to my tent and threw my stuff down on a cot, the guy next to me made a comment that I was very close to his cot. I apologized but told him we'd be cramped because we had ten more people coming in at 4 a.m. and another twenty or so the following morning. He seemed weird about it. I knew him from the other site, and he had really liked me back there. As a matter of fact I had helped him pass his physical training (PT) test. So I was surprised by his attitude but also wondered if I was just overreacting. I finally moved my cot away from his because he kept going on and on, commenting that he was worried about being sick and he hadn't been sick the whole time. I finally started to get pissed and said, "I'm sorry, buddy, there's nothing I can do." He remarked on how they had tried to get the officers another place to live, but that had failed. Then he mentioned that our heads shouldn't face the same direction in our cots. This might have been legitimate, but the way he said it made me feel very unwelcome. So I finally snapped at him: "Do what you need to do. I'm gonna lay my shit here."

I hope he was genuinely concerned about germs, but it seemed strange for a guy who had been in the army for years to all of a sudden be concerned about sleeping next to a soldier in close living quarters. Was I overreacting, or had I just encountered someone who was freaked out about me? Normally gay folks come out to a handful of people closest to them. In my case it was like someone had taken a huge scalpel and gouged out this cancer that had been inside of me without giving me anything to numb the pain. I had no option but to face it head on. It's the only way to change people's way of thinking and the culture of the army.

Later, one night at supper with my buddy Renshaw, a bunch of civilian contractors sat down beside us. I am not sure if any of them recognized me, but they kept looking over and started talking about fags in the military and fags in the showers. I had to restrain myself. I didn't know if they were doing it to screw with me or if they were just unlucky that I was sitting there. I was worried that if I confronted them, Renshaw and I might get into a fight, so I sat there and just listened. Later Renshaw told me that it really pissed him off. It amazes me when homophobic people assume gay people are attracted to them by default; it is usually quite the opposite.

This is probably the worst interaction I experienced since the repeal, and it didn't even involve U.S. soldiers, just some civilian contractors working sixty days on and thirty days off, making a couple hundred thousand U.S. taxpayer dollars. So I was basically paying their salary to eat free food and call me a fag. Nice. Contractors were not required to go through DADT repeal training, but maybe they should have been. It makes me proud to be a soldier knowing our men and women in uniform have been much more professional, and many would stand up for me against homophobic thugs like that.

That night, while we were eating supper, the news was highlighting a *Saturday Night Live* skit that showed Rick Santorum at a gay bar, bumping into people like crazy. One of my friends laughed and told me that was probably happening to Santorum because of the Republican debates. That was a lot to process: Could I have been responsible for people making fun of his antigay stance?

UNITED STATES ARMY
CERTIFICATE OF ENLISTMENT
THIS IS TO CERTIFY THAT

PRIVATE STEPHEN M. HILL

HAS ENLISTED FOR SERVICE IN THE UNITED STATES ARMY

As a new member of the Army, you have demonstrated keen foresight by accepting the Army's challenge. You can be justly proud of your decision to enlist in the Army for service to your nation. The people of the United States are deeply grateful to you for your personal commitment to national defense.

8 NOVEMBER 1988

DATE

NICHOLAS J. HUN
LTC, MP
Commanding

USAREC Fm 569, Rev 1 Apr 85 (Previous editions are obsolete)

1. (*above*) My enlistment certificate from 1988, signifying the beginning of my military career.

2. (*left*) The drill sergeants "smoked us" right before our basic training picture, so I had just done a bunch of pushups and run before this picture was taken.

3. My basic training platoon. I'm in the third row up, fourth from the right.

4. Writing in my journal in Iraq. Having that journal stolen was one of the biggest losses I have ever encountered.

5. During Desert Storm I had soot from burning oil wells all over my face all the time.

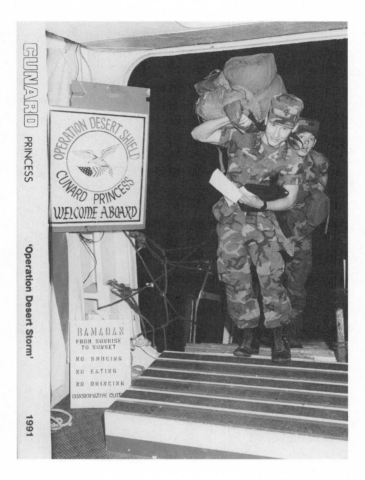

6. Boarding the *Cunard Princess*, the beginning of being lost in Iraq.

7. Taken at the Dachau Concentration Camp Memorial Site, this photo will always mean a lot to me. I took the picture not knowing what the pink triangles meant, but remembering these prison uniforms later had a huge impact on my life. A picture is worth a thousand words.

8. This was taken after my promotion to captain in 2006.

9. You do get to travel in the army. During Operation Bright Star I got to go on a morale welfare and recreation (MWR) trip to see the pyramids.

10. Premobilization training in Seattle before leaving for Iraq in November of 2010.

11. (*left, above*) Josh and me after we were legally married at the grave of Leonard Matlovich, while I was on R&R leave from Iraq, about four months prior to the repeal of "Don't Ask, Don't Tell." This was the happiest day of my life.

12. (*left, below*) This is our marriage certificate. It lists the Congressional Cemetery as our wedding site.

13. (*above*) I came out to millions instantaneously as I asked my question during the Republican presidential debate on September 22, 2011.

14. (*above*) Rachel Maddow covered my story several times on her show, and Josh and I got to meet her when we were in New York.

15. (*below*) Josh and I met Admiral Mike Mullen, giving me the opportunity to look him in the eye to tell him how much it meant to me that he had risked his career and reputation to testify that gay people could serve without affecting the military's readiness. Photo courtesy of Chris Burch.

16. (*above*) Thomas Roberts from MSNBC covered my story many times on his show.

17. (*below*) Josh and I were highlighted at the Logo New Now Next Awards, where we got to meet Andrew Rannells, star of TV's *The New Normal*.

18. (*above*) The C-BUS of Love. This was taken just five days before the Supreme Court ruled on DOMA.

19. (*below*) Josh and I were selected to be grand marshals of the Columbus Pride Parade. You can see all of the newlyweds behind us.

20. (*above*) Our family: Josh, me, Macho, and Gizmo. Photo courtesy of Logan McWilliams.

21. (*below*) Josh and me with our hometown of Columbus, Ohio, in the background. Photo courtesy of Amy Ann Photography.

22. Josh with his military ID. He is finally recognized as my husband by the military.

13 The Lawsuit

Watching human rights evolve is a bit like watching hermit crabs race. The pace is pretty slow, and sometimes the crabs turn around and scamper backward a bit before rediscovering their forward momentum. The repeal of DADT was a major leap in the human rights race for gay soldiers, but the military's (and the federal government's) refusal to recognize gay marriages remained a stubborn, backward-facing crab. It all hinged on the Defense of Marriage Act (DOMA).

Signed into law in 1996 by then-president Bill Clinton, DOMA defined marriage as the legal union between one man and one woman. It prevented the federal government from recognizing same-sex marriages, even if they were performed in a state where same-sex marriage is legal. Under the law no state was required to recognize a same-sex marriage from another state, and same-sex couples were excluded from the federal benefits afforded to heterosexual married couples. DOMA was intended to circumvent states' laws, but the worst part is that creating a law that defines marriage as between a man and a woman seems to integrate religion into the law. The irony is that this is the opposite of what America was founded on.

The scary thing is, where does it stop? If you want to integrate religious principles into American politics, then do so by treating your neighbor as you expect to be treated. But if you want to take the question more literally, then the religious freedom upon which our nation was founded will find itself in serious jeopardy. A lot of conservatives are selective about how they examine religious doctrine. There are crazy examples in the Bible of things we are supposed to do and not do—don't wear clothes of mixed fibers, don't touch a woman who is menstruating, don't shave, not to even mention the acceptance of slavery. Which other ones should we integrate into the law? I am no legal expert, but it's a slippery slope. And that's the reason separation of church and state exists in the first place.

The military used DOMA as the reason it would not provide benefits to same-sex spouses. The military stated that we are federal employees who have to follow federal law. Meanwhile in 2009 President Barack Obama signed a memorandum granting some benefits to the same-sex partners of federal (State Department) employees. These employees are governed under the same law, so why did DOMA discriminate against me and not them?

That is why I was interested to hear what OutServe had to say when they contacted me in Iraq about a class-action lawsuit, *McLaughlin vs. Panetta*, that would challenge DOMA. OutServe, a social media group for actively serving LGBT soldiers, began as a secret Facebook group launched in 2010 by an anonymous person who went by the name of JD Smith. OutServe was looking for legally married gay and lesbian soldiers to participate in the lawsuit, which would be filed at the end of October, a little more than a month before I got off of active duty. The Servicemembers Legal Defense Network (SLDN) and Chadborne & Park represented some soldiers who decided to pursue the lawsuit, and they used OutServe as a conduit to contact Josh and me.

Many of the soldiers who had been discharged over the years of "Don't Ask, Don't Tell" were directed to contact SLDN, a collection of lawyers who worked together to offer free legal services to servicemembers. I first learned about the SLDN while reading a *Stars and Stripes* article published months before the repeal of DADT. From the title of the organization I would have never known it had anything to do with gay people. Maybe that was the original intent.

More than fourteen thousand servicemembers were discharged under DADT because of their sexual orientation. Since its founding in 1993 SLDN has responded to more than twelve thousand requests for assistance. The organization has given discharged servicemembers legal guidance, assisted with litigation, and helped them submit paperwork to try to stay in the military or negotiate the type of discharge they received. A lot of its revenue came through donations. I can only assume that during "Don't Ask, Don't Tell" donations were probably very strong, as many people realized that this organization was the only alternative that gay servicemen and servicewomen had. Representative Patrick Murphy introduced the bill that would ultimately repeal DADT, but SLDN and its team were the powerhouse that was instrumental in working with Capitol Hill to make repeal a reality.

At the time we joined the lawsuit, I was the only plaintiff currently deployed. Josh made a trip to Washington DC, where he met the staff of SLDN and the other plaintiffs, including Charlie Morgan. Charlie epitomized everything we had been and still are fighting for. At the time Josh met her, she had just returned from a year of serving her country, only to be diagnosed with stage-4 breast cancer. Time was short for her and her family: her wife, Karen, and their child, Casey. Out of all the plaintiffs Josh met, he connected with Charlie the most. He told me her story and described what a wonderful person she was.

Besides Charlie, Josh also talked about Aubrey Sarvis, the director of and brains behind SLDN, and Zeke Stokes, the media director who coached Josh through his first interview on MSNBC. My first epiphany about how big all this was on the outside came after watching the HBO documentary *The Strange History of Don't Ask, Don't Tell* in Iraq. The film followed the staff of SLDN during the steps to repeal and everything that happened behind the scenes. All of a sudden I was watching on TV the people Josh was interacting with on a daily basis. It was surreal.

A friend in the army who came out to me after the debates introduced me to a couple of lesbians. One of them thanked me once she realized I was the one making all the headlines. I told her about the lawsuit, and she seemed to tear up a little. When I probed a bit to find out why, she told me how mad she was that she couldn't bring her partner to yellow ribbon ceremonies. The unit said she could pay for her partner's trip, but they'd still have to list her as "single." This policy excluded the couple from a lot of the things that are supposed to strengthen the bond between a servicemember and his or her mate. Such ceremonies are also supposed to help repair any damage that might have occurred as the result of deployment. The military holds "Strong Bonds" retreats, and gay people can go, but we have to go as single. Even after the repeal and the fall of DOMA, gay people are still not invited to these. This woman even told me that this exclusion had created animosity between her and her spouse, so instead of being a strengthening tool for their relationship, this ceremony was now a barrier.

She also told me that the day before the repeal of DADT, she went to the gym and heard people trying to outdo one another with the number of times they could say the words *faggot* and *queer*. It was a big joke to them because this was the last day they were allowed to mock us with derogatory comments. Talking the talk and walking the walk are two different things. It was easy to get on TV and get national attention for asking a question, but facing my fellow soldiers out in the open in the midst of a lawsuit would be quite different. I was getting a little exhausted, worrying this lawsuit would create even more hype. But her story completely renewed my faith and my fight for gay servicemembers to enjoy the same rights as our heterosexual counterparts. It made me want to fight harder.

Leonard Matlovich started this fight back when I was a little kid. Now I want to finish it. He paved the way for me to have the freedom to serve my country openly and with dignity. I hope that by exposing the hatred several Republican candidates made central to their campaign, I cemented the right for gay people to serve in the military and never go back. I hope that by being a good soldier, an example of a gay person who serves, I can break people's stereotypes. This is a fight against bigotry, and it succeeds one person at a time. Every day I see how one person can make a difference.

Before I knew it, media releases on Facebook were reporting that SLDN was going to file a huge lawsuit but declined to expose who the plaintiffs were. I was worried because I knew the press would be looking for the names, and it wouldn't take them long to find mine, put two and two together, and realize that I was the person from the Republican debates. That made me think this thing might really be blown out of proportion. Out of professional courtesy I needed to tell my commander, once again.

I had already put my unit through the debate and the fallout, so I was worried about adding to the pile. First I went to our command sergeant major. We had been pretty close throughout the deployment, and I felt like he always had my back. Right after the debates aired, he had joked with me, "I can't go any damn where around this place without seeing your face on TV!" He might have been partially serious, but all things considered, he took the lawsuit pretty well. I mean, it's not every day that you tell your command you're suing the Department of Defense. Of course, we were not really suing the army; we were bringing suit against DOMA. He instructed me to go to the commander, since she might be required to inform her chain of command that a lawsuit was about to be filed on my behalf (and that of the other plaintiffs). I made an appointment with her.

I had very limited access to the Internet, so I had a hard time knowing what was going on back home. Once I was finally able to sign on, I found a message from Josh that I needed to contact him ASAP. The date for the lawsuit had been set for October 27, 2011, and SLDN was flying Josh out to Washington DC to be interviewed by the media. The timing of all of this was insane: that was the date I would be either in the final countdown to leave or already on the plane headed to Seattle for postmobilization training. Since Josh would be in Washington, and they would say he was the husband of a deployed soldier, I knew that the identity of that "deployed soldier" would come out, and then all hell would break loose.

The night of the conference call about the lawsuit between SLDN and all of the plaintiffs, one of my friends at the unit got a message that his dad had died. The army was working with the Red Cross to get him home. This again reminded me that if something were to happen to my husband, it was unlikely that I'd be notified, and even if I were, I wouldn't be allowed to grieve and attend his funeral because DOMA prevented the military from recognizing him as my immediate family. What if I couldn't go home and bury my husband? This was a hard reality, and it made me want to fight harder.

The 27th came quickly. Josh went live on MSNBC. It was weird because even though I had appeared on just about every news station, I had never actually been *on* them. Being interviewed by Al Sharpton is a lot of pressure, so I felt a little sorry for Josh. They flew him out and had him answer a bunch of questions in a preinterview. Then they threw him in front of a camera. You could tell he was nervous. During the clip Al pretty much read Josh's answers to him on TV, basically leaving him with nothing to say. MSNBC showed the clip from the GOP debates and asked him what he thought about the booing. Josh didn't emphasize the booing at all. In fact he said we hadn't even noticed it.

When the interview was over, I Skyped Josh and scolded him (though I felt bad about this later) for saying this because the booing was significant for me. Then he explained how he had experienced the whole event versus what I had seen on TV, and that made me realize we were in very different places. The bottom line was that Josh was proud we had gotten the question out and exposed the bigotry. Josh continued to do several more interviews, some radio spots, and even some local news stories. I really liked one of the radio interviews because he talked about the mortar hit and his worry about what would take place if something happened to me.

The irony of all this was that I was sitting in Iraq on a time-controlled army Morale, Welfare, and Recreation (MWR) computer. I only had ten minutes to email and surf the web. I searched for the clip with Josh. Mind you, this was after the debates, but it was also after our units had consolidated, so I wasn't as recognizable as "the booed soldier." I didn't have my headphones with me, so as I listened to the interview through the external speakers, the repetition of the word *gay* still had me feeling paranoid. It's hard to get rid of that self-preservation instinct. I was still worried people would hear and judge me. DADT was over. I had been on national TV, and I had become a plaintiff in a lawsuit against the Department of Defense. I thought to myself, why am I lowering the volume? To this day I think this whole policy still has the crazy effect of making people look over their shoulder and worry what others think.

14 Prepping for the Public Eye

The day finally came when we boarded a flight back to the United States of America. There are no words that can articulate how it feels when you come home from serving your country after a year at war. This was a curious time for me because while one chapter in my life was getting ready to close, another huge one was unraveling. The one thing that made me chuckle as I quietly sat in my seat was this thought: not one motherfucker will get on the PA and make fun of gay people now. I smiled and peacefully fell asleep.

Shortly after we arrived in Seattle, the television network NBC contacted the army to find out my information. Our s-1 person (staff officer) informed me that I was being asked to do interviews and asked if I wanted to engage the media now or wait until I was processed off of active duty. I would still be on active duty until sometime in December, and in the military there are very specific rules about talking to the media if you are on active duty. The reserves are a little more lenient. It's not like I would ever say something unprofessional; it's just more comfortable knowing you're not under quite as much scrutiny. My message was (and still is) very simple and clear: I am a soldier. Treat me the same way you treat other soldiers, same conduct rules, no special treatment, no favors, no different considerations. This was all new territory for me, a foreshadowing of events to come.

The s-1 arranged for the PAO (public affairs officer) from the army to meet with me to talk about the situation and engagement of the media. This was a big deal because it was the first formal communication from the army about what I should and shouldn't say to the media, and it really was my first feedback about what had happened, so needless to say I was nervous. I was sitting in an auditorium when my commander tapped me on the shoulder to let me know that a colonel was there from the PAO. I turned around and saw a tall man in a uniform. When I first learned I had to talk to someone from the PAO, I had envisioned a really mean, angry person coming to confront me. I was scared and had no idea what to expect, but he seemed polite and offered to go off-site to discuss what the army had to say about the incident.

He drove me out for coffee and started to engage, but it seemed like neither of us knew how to start talking about the whole thing. He seemed interested in why I had done what I did, so I shared most of what is in this book with him. We talked for hours, taking our conversation from morning coffee into a lunch meeting. He mostly listened, always seeming fascinated by these stories of what LGBT soldiers have endured. Toward the end of the day he disclosed to me that he had a twenty-one-year-old son who had recently come out to him. He said he had grown up in a "macho" world and didn't know how to relate to his son, but he told me that talking to me was helpful.

I stopped him midsentence and said, "If you think you know your son better now, I am going to blow your mind . . . stick with me on this one. You know all that conditioning and mindset changing you had to go through to deprogram what society taught you to think about gay people, in this 'macho' way you were raised?"

"Yeah," he said, waiting for me to continue.

"Imagine this—your son went through all of that too," I said. "He also has to deprogram himself out of thinking it's bad, out of hating himself, into accepting and eventually maybe even loving himself. People don't realize that when people finally admit to themselves that they're gay, they also have to unlearn all that crap about who they have to be or how they have to act."

He looked like a light bulb had gone off in his head. He was blown away, and I could tell that I had won him over by telling my story. We were supposed to spend only an hour or two together. His job was to give me guidance on how to interact with the media and be professional, as well as how sound bites work. For the most part he did that, but we ended up spending the entire day together. When I told him I wanted to write a book (this book) about my experiences, he was the first person to really encourage me to do that. He drove me back, and I will never forget his words.

"Captain Hill, you have two choices," he said. "You can let this thing die out. You can choose not to engage the media, and it will fizzle away. Or you can engage them and tell your story."

He paused, and I had no idea what would come out of his mouth next.

"I feel it would be a tragedy for you to not tell this story," he continued. "It was very compelling to hear what you have told me today and a good army story."

He told me it was an incredible story that a lot of people could learn from. He said that "Don't Ask, Don't Tell" was in the past, that I was a good soldier, and that soon people would realize how this policy was not benefiting the army. Later I sat in my room and thought hard about what he had said. Then I began writing this book.

The soldiers in the army continue to surprise me. Not only did they react wonderfully after the debate, but the officer they sent to prep me for the media was understanding about my situation and actually encouraged me to follow my heart. After so many negative experiences and having to hide and lie about myself for so many years, I am so amazed that a representative from the army told me to be proud of myself and tell my story to people. This is what reengages everything that DADT took away from me. I believe in my country. I believe in my freedom, and just like Chris Matthews would later tell me, the good guys always win in the end. My interaction with the PAO really energized me to become a stronger fighter for liberty and equality, and to me this has always been what "being a soldier" means. It also taught me the most important lesson about being a soldier of change: you have to tell your story.

Later, as things were revving up, Josh did an interview with our local news. The station tried to do responsible journalism by offering an opposing view, one that held that gay people should not have their marriages recognized by the military. The story was about us suing for equal benefits, so naturally I think an opposing view should have been someone from the military explaining the policy, which says that equal benefits can't be provided under DOMA. Instead they brought in Linda Harvey from a crazy conservative group called Mission America, which is part of the "pray the gay away" movement. They went from Josh to her voiceover about how gay people are immoral and our behavior is unacceptable to her. I guess this was the first time we received a personal attack from someone interviewed by the media. This took me right back to that OSU seminar on praying the gay away; it infuriated me.

It bothered me because Linda Harvey will never be affected by me; she will never know me or probably ever exchange two words with me. I am still trying to figure out why people hate and constantly try to oppress people they don't even know. They don't want me to marry, even though it has no impact on their life. I guess that if same-sex marriage ever becomes legal nationwide, the people who hate us might worry we'll have lower rates of divorce or spousal abuse, and that will be threatening. Other than that, I just can't figure out why people care. So when she says it is a moral issue, she might do more research to find out what my morals are and not judge me for being one of "those people."

As the time for coming home was drawing closer, Josh was telling me that SLDN was lining up a bunch of media interviews. One of the things about being deployed is that you have to reintegrate into your life on return. You need to adjust back into your normal routine. I was getting a little anxious because I didn't know what I was going to come back to. What was normal for me at this point? Having the media interview me—that was not normal. So I was telling Josh I wasn't sure I wanted to talk to anyone at this point. I was starting to feel like I didn't want this to take over my life, and I didn't want it to become more important than reintegrating. I really missed the life that I had been absent from over the last year, and I needed to recover.

We continued our demobilization process in Seattle. At one station I had to review my life insurance. The woman processing my paperwork paused as she stared down at the sheet.

"I can't sign off; we have to stamp yours," she said.

I asked her why, though I knew it was because I had named Josh, my "friend," as my beneficiary if I were killed.

"Because your beneficiary is unconventional," she said.

Now, with the repeal of "Don't Ask, Don't Tell," just like Superman deflecting a bullet off of his chest, I said, "Not at all, because he is my husband; the army just makes me list him as a friend."

I would never have dreamed over my twenty years in the military that I'd ever be able to say those words. When I was getting ready to be deployed, I was so nervous to list Josh as a friend on the application. And now I had no problem calling him my husband. But the coolest part is that another soldier who was sitting beside me said, "That is messed up, that you have to list him as a friend and get stamped off." He sounded sincerely upset by this, like he wanted to fight for me.

"Well, I'm working to change that," I told him. "I hope that one day the army will recognize my marriage."

I loved the support I was getting from my fellow soldiers. This moment reminds me of a comic I saw online the other day that shows two soldiers sitting in a foxhole during combat. One of the soldiers is showing a picture to the other one, and he says, "This is my boyfriend back home. I hope we make it out of here alive so I can find a state that will let us get married."

My newfound "infamy" could have been uncomfortable with the soldiers in my unit, but humor helped all of us find a common bond. For example, if one of the soldiers did something the rest of us didn't like, such as make us wait to get on a bus, someone would yell out, "Boo that man!" and everyone would boo. Then I'd usually yell at them, "Don't boo soldiers; that's not right!" It was a universal acknowledgment of how crazy it was for those people at the debate to boo me. And it seemed to make our unit stronger, so the argument about gay soldiers destroying unit cohesiveness is definitely false.

Another example was a time I was on baggage detail with a bunch of soldiers in Iraq, the first time I had been with such a big group since the debate. We were all throwing bags out of a five-ton vehicle. All the bags are army green, so people tie stuff to their bag to make it easily identifiable. I picked up a bag that had a big rainbow ribbon wrapped around it and glanced up. All the other soldiers were looking at me in silence. So I stopped what I was doing, smiled at all of them, and said, "Just for the record . . . this is *not* my bag!" Everyone burst out in laughter, and after that people were much easier to talk to. It loosened everyone up and made them realize that I was the same person. They thought it was funny and realized it doesn't have to be such a serious topic.

So everything was going great with the people I was currently serving with, but there was still a big group of soldiers back home who hadn't been deployed with our group. I wondered what their reaction would be upon my return. While in Seattle I received a call from SFC Rennicker, the noncommissioned officer from our section. He told me some of the soldiers in my section were a little nervous that I wouldn't be the same, that I would be stuffy or maybe a bleeding-heart activist. I joked with him and told him we had to paint the walls of our section pink when I got home. He laughed. Yet again humor proved to be the best tension breaker. Rennicker is a great leader. He understood this situation was tense for some people, and he took the initiative and did what he does best: he led. To this day he is one of my strongest supporters and a great example of the professionalism that is ingrained in the military.

He spread the word that I was the exact same person as I had been before Iraq, and a group followed up with a phone call once I got home. It was their drill weekend, so they were all in town, and they invited me to come have a beer with them. That meant a lot to me because it was an attempt to reach out and show me that things between us were not different. These were the same guys I used to lie to, and one of them was the guy who had told me my house looked like "a gay dude's" house. So the invitation was kind of a healing thing for me and made me feel welcome to come back.

We finally got our flights scheduled to travel home. I had so much anticipation to see Josh and my family. Josh had adopted another dog, Gizmo, right after my R&R, so I was excited to meet my new family member. I arrived at the airport, and along with the time I returned from Desert Storm, every detail of coming home will be etched in my mind forever. Both of our sets of parents were waiting for me. My mother-in-law was so cute: she didn't realize her "welcome home" sign with a flag was turned upside-down.

When I walked into my house, I had to fight the urge to cry because it was over; it was all finally over. The first night I slept in Iraq, I remember thinking, *Only 407 more nights to go*, and that seemed like an eternity ago. I finally sat in my home with my puppy, Macho, crazily licking my face, holding back my tears of joy.

Veterans Day was right around the corner. Soldiers were invited to be in the parade, but I was asked to walk with the Stonewall Veterans. This was the first time since the repeal of DADT that gay people had marched openly in a Veterans Day parade. For some reason I was very nervous. We marched down the road, unsure how people would react to our rainbow flag waving front and center next to the POW flag and, of course, Old Glory. But people clapped and yelled out "thank you." It was such an empowering experience. Lots of thank yous. To me this was a testimony of what America really felt (the same America that scorned the boos from the audience in the Republican debate).

Josh had been secretly planning a welcome-home benefit for me, complete with a bunch of entertainers (some drag queens, some speakers). At first I was opposed to it, especially when I saw the poster that read, "Featuring Captain Stephen Hill." I didn't want this to be about me, so I told Josh I didn't want to go unless they mentioned all of the veterans. He promised it would be okay. We went in, and the place was pretty packed. The support from the Columbus gay community amazed me. They kicked off the night by showing many of the news clips, which was cool. Then the Capital Pride Band of Columbus played "The Star-Spangled Banner." The whole night was a reunion of sorts, or maybe it was something out of *This Is Your Life*. One of the band members was Marc, the sociology student from OSU who was first person I had ever come out to. Keith, the first guy I had ever dated, also flew in from California. Even my cousin Bobby and his wife showed up.

Josh got up and said a few words, thanking everyone for their service. He also reminded people there were many things that still threatened us as a community, so we could not stop fighting for our rights and freedom, and we could never be comfortable with status quo. He reminded people that we lived in a bubble and not to forget where we still stood. This was the first time

I really saw in Josh's eyes that he had changed over the year I was gone. He was no longer someone to sit on the sidelines and quietly advocate for equality. He had become a leader, standing right up front and demanding equal rights.

Following the drag show, which was fun, they showed a video of my family and several other people welcoming me home. Then they announced, "In a minute we will hear from Captain Hill." I didn't know I was going to be speaking. As I slid my chair out from the table and looked around at everyone there, the anxiety quickly went away, and for a moment I started to feel like a leader. It felt like all the people in that room needed someone to advocate for them, and they were grateful I was willing to do so. The most important thing I said to them was that this was not about me, not at all. This was about and for every gay servicemember who used to have to serve his or her country in silence. I clenched my fists. *No more.* I then asked my two friends who were just off of deployment and another veteran I knew in the audience to stand up. I said, "This is for them, to never have to lie to serve their country again." I paused, looked around again, and repeated: "*Never again.*" The room erupted in thunderous applause. The leader inside of me started to emerge.

The first week I was back, someone said they had seen an article about the lawsuit in our local newspaper. We ran out to grab a paper and read the story, which offered a brief version of my story and an outline of the legal battle against DOMA. The paper did a pretty nice job with the story, but we were a little perplexed by the term "gay pairs" in the title. That seemed weird, like they didn't know what to call us, but the story was good. Later we got a call from SLDN, and they said the Associated Press would be the agency to do my official first interview since returning. I wanted Josh to be part of it. The Associated Press contacted me and said they would send out someone to do a video interview, then later a photographer, and then someone would do the phone interview for print.

The photographer came out first. He asked questions, and I answered, but he wasn't part of the interview. So it basically seemed like I was providing sound bites. The last question he asked was, "You are a gay icon; how does that feel?" I answered, but his question bothered me, as I didn't feel like a gay icon, and I didn't want this to be about me. This was about all the men and women serving our country. When the clip was edited, they only played my response to his question, so it sounded like the "gay icon" comment had come from me, and I didn't like that.

Despite that, the photographer took some nice photos of Josh and me. I loved that. Then later we spent an hour and a half on a phone interview with the reporter who wrote the story. She was great. The actual print job was very nice and representative.

Unfortunately, not everything was great about the release of my first story. Our local paper picked up the AP story but edited it by cutting out two paragraphs from the original story in which I specified that the political and legal fight was not about sex or conduct and that I was most upset that a presidential candidate had defined my marriage and military service in those terms. Our local paper has always been conservative, but it was hurtful to me that they edited out the most important piece of the entire story, when I said, "I'm fighting every day to protect everyone's rights as human beings, and it seems counterintuitive for me to be fighting for those rights and not have them." What they cut out changed the entire meaning of my fight. So I wrote a letter to the editor and posted a comment on their website about how my own hometown newspaper was the *only* paper out of 191 news organizations that had picked up the story to change and edit it. I was tired of people censoring my life. That comment not only got them to change the story and add the edited content but also gained the attention of some local filmmakers. More about that later.

Our lawsuit continued in litigation. We started to slowly

see results of our efforts. One of the most significant results of negotiations during the SLDN suit was that we were permitted for the first time to bring our same-sex spouses to the army's yellow ribbon event. I immediately registered to take my parents and Josh.

Yellow ribbon events are held before and after deployments. Your family is invited, and people from the military talk about some of the things you might experience during deployment. They also give very good debriefings to families after deployment. Josh actually got to attend this one (one of the first same-sex spouses to do so). He found it informative, as they talked about some of the stuff he had experienced as the spouse of a soldier. Of course they didn't address the additional stress on an LGBT spouse, which is an entire different ballgame.

It was a lovely event, held in Denver. Everyone was respectful, a funny observation that shows my years of conditioning: I considered it a success because no one treated me like shit or made a hateful comment. I hope that with time we will all heal. We had a nice time, and the army provided some good information to my family. But it was still frustrating to hear them talk about the family benefits, like "Strong Bonds" retreats, that were still not offered to my family. These are special military-sanctioned vacations for a husband and "wife." They are centered on counseling and getting to know one another or strengthening your relationship. They have traditionally originated from the chaplain's office, so even to this day inviting same-sex couples has not been discussed. This is still an inequity in the military. I hope that with the fall of DOMA eventually something will happen with the "Strong Bonds" events too. Gay relationships are every bit as vulnerable to deployment. So in one way it was awesome that Josh could attend, but in another it was like dangling a carrot in front of our faces. They were still saying, "This is for them, not you."

While we were there, we did a long interview with the

Denver NBC news affiliate. One thing you realize when you get interviewed by lots of media is that you never know how a story will turn out until it gets published. I spent the majority of the interview talking about our lawsuit, about how it was not just monetary but for things like family leave if one of us were killed. So after a forty-minute discussion and interview with the reporters the footage got chopped up to make it sound like I was only interested in the monetary portion . . . ugh. I was slowly learning the proper way to engage with the media. This was not about money; it was about human rights.

15 Did Rosa Parks Have a Roommate?

After you come home from deployment, you have up to ninety days to return to your civilian job. I decided to take a month off after my leave was up. That would get me through the holidays I had missed the previous year. In January, I went back to work. Reacclimating to my civilian job was a little rough. People take for granted how much you miss when you're away. They expect you to jump back in, know everything that happened while you were gone, and be fully functional. You go through such difficult life changes, but then jumping back into a job you haven't done for a year is yet another huge life change. Columbus Public Health hosted a nice welcome-home party for me, which lots of people attended, thanking me for my service. The health commissioner and our veterans' coordinator presented me with a letter from the mayor of Columbus, Michael Coleman. I talked briefly to our staff and thanked everyone.

A couple of weeks later I received a call from the mayor's office. He invited my boss and me to join him and his veterans' coordinator in a meeting. It started out mostly as a conversation about what I do for the army, and both men thanked me for my service. Then the veterans' coordinator said, pointing to me, "Mayor, he is fighting the good fight against DOMA." That opened up a dialogue for me with our mayor, who had never publicly taken a stance on gay marriage.

My mission was not to change his mind that day; I simply wanted to tell him my experiences. I told him about "Red,

White and Boom," about protecting everyone's freedom except my own, and about hiding pictures in my own house to serve my country. I talked about the debate. I talked a long time about my marriage to Josh. Then I pointed to my ring and said, "You know, Mayor, *this* is not recognized in Ohio yet."

"No, it isn't, but that would take an act of Congress," he replied.

"No, it takes one person at a time," I said. I think my story was compelling to him. He had sons who served in the military, and I think my story caused him to think a lot about each soldier's personal story. The strongest and most powerful thing you can do to advocate for change is to tell your story. When you talk about social issues, whether women's reproductive rights, abortion, or gay marriage—I think a personal story makes all the difference in the world in changing opinions.

Two days later the *Columbus Dispatch* ran a story about the mayor's intention to sign on with the Mayors for the Freedom to Marry and the Ohio Leaders for Freedom to Marry. In the story the mayor cited our conversation as the thing that had pushed him over the top. This was actually the first time I felt like I really was making a difference. I received a call the next day from the mayor's office, inviting Josh and me to the "State of the City" address, during which the mayor might talk about his decision and about courage and change. The mayor's cabinet wanted to know if I would be willing to be there while he used my story as an example. How exciting, I thought, and I agreed.

The event was amazing and extremely well attended. Mayor Coleman introduced me as an example of courage. He told my story, about how the leaders at the debate had turned their backs on me. Then he told everyone that the City of Columbus saluted me and would not turn its back on me. He asked me to stand up, and when I did, they shone a spotlight on me. Everyone applauded. I happened to be seated behind the police officers and firefighters, many of whom turned around to shake my hand. One even gave me a salute. How amazing!

A few months later the City of Columbus presented legislation for a Domestic Partner Registry. First the mayor had publicly endorsed marriage equality, and now it seemed like Columbus kept opening up to new ways to support gay people. We were so excited at this small step. I think little things like these send a big message to Washington. So even though Josh and I were already married, we wanted to register with the city. We had to support all efforts to bring about equality!

We didn't announce to anyone we were coming; we just decided it was important to be there the day the registry opened. Looking back, we wished we had gotten there earlier, just for the bragging rights of being the first registered domestic partners in Columbus. When the time is right, we'll make sure to camp out to have our marriage be the first one registered in Ohio.

At the ceremony Councilman Zach Kline, who had introduced the legislation for the registry, delivered his remarks while looking into the audience. But then he looked at me and said, "And I see a veteran who has given so much to his country. This is our way of giving back." I have paraphrased what he said, but he really was saying the same thing that I had told the mayor when I met with him: that for my entire military life I had felt like I was fighting for everyone's freedom and rights . . . except my own.

We also received some other really good news around this time, that the Department of Justice had sent a letter to the Speaker of the House stating it would not defend DOMA when it came to military personnel. This was an exciting break in our case and a very positive step in the right direction. SLDN executive director Aubrey Sarvis issued the following statement: "We are pleased that the Attorney General has decided not to defend the constitutionality of DOMA in the military context, just as he has declined to defend it in other contexts. We are also delighted that, for the first time, he has said that separate definitions that apply to military veterans are also unconstitutional. This is an important step for the McLaughlin plaintiffs."

My life started to turn upside-down because the more we got invested in fighting for our rights, the more passionate we became. Sometimes I look back and think about how all the stars aligned for things to work out like they have to give Josh and me so many opportunities to be activists for equality. Sometimes it seems like a one-in-a-million chance that it worked out like it did. One of those times again involved our local paper. Up to this point, out of all the online comments about myself I had been reading since the debates—both positive and negative—I had never responded to any of them (mostly because SLDN told me not to). But I had to speak up once I saw how the local paper hacked up my AP article. Then, after posting my comment about the story, I received an email from a college student who was doing a film project on gay rights and the effort to bring about marriage equality in Ohio. He asked if we would agree to appear in the documentary, which would be shown at the Drexel theater. He was so excited that he had found me through that article, which was fate because I had not posted on anything else. He couldn't believe I was local: he knew about the debate but had no idea I lived in Ohio, much less Columbus.

The film crew came to our home with an entire entourage and lots of equipment. My house looked like a movie studio. Between the dogs barking at every passerby and our roommate, Adam, walking in, filming was a bit of a mess. For a while, at the height of our media engagement, we seemed to be interviewed every week for follow-up stories about the debate or our activism. Adam joked that every time he came home, he found someone interviewing or filming us. At one point he said, "I always wondered if Rosa Parks had a roommate." I thought that was really funny, but it also gave me pause. Does anyone who makes a change in the world ever know they are doing it while it is happening? Maybe Rosa Parks and I have a lot in common. It dawned on me that I really identify with her. She was probably this sweet woman who just got really pissed off one day. She probably said, "Hey, screw this, I am done being treated like trash, and I have every right to sit where you sit." I pictured myself doing the same thing. I realized that standing up for yourself and pointing out the obvious wrong all of a sudden becomes a crystal-clear heroic act.

I started to read more about her out of curiosity. I learned that she was in her forties when the incident on the bus occurred. I had always envisioned her as a warrior who had trained her whole life to fight for what she believed in. But in reality she was a normal human being; she worked at hospitals, as a seamstress, and in other commonplace jobs. But by chance one of her actions changed the world. Reading about her life made me realize that even "normal" human beings have the power to make changes in this world.

We started regularly attending various events to advocate for gay rights and marriage equality. We were asked to speak at a Marriage Equality Rally in Cleveland, so Josh and I agreed to drive up there. Using the Internet to organize the rally, a teenager named Adam was able to gather about three thousand people, including former congresswoman Mary Jo Kilroy. This was right after she had lost an election, so for her to show up with no motivation other than to demonstrate support made a huge statement. What an incredible testimony of a politician really representing her constituents (even after they hadn't reelected her). I admire her.

They introduced us, and I started to talk. I told them Josh and I were married, and everyone cheered. I interrupted them to say, "But this means nothing here in Ohio . . . and this is why we are all here today." Thunderous applause again.

Josh spoke and did a great job. He noted how people were *evolving*. Again I saw the new leader in him as he spoke. I think this is what planted the seed in his head for a new project. He said, "Today a line is drawn in the sand; you are either on the right side of history, or you are not." People cheered, and it was awesome. By the time we got home, someone had already put the video of our speeches online, complete with a compelling soundtrack. This publicity and momentum seemed unreal, and to this day it still shocks me.

When the annual SLDN fundraising dinner came around, we were invited as plaintiffs in the case. But since the SLDN had done so much for me, especially in their efforts to repeal "Don't Ask, Don't Tell," we decided to purchase tickets anyway to support them. At the dinner they introduced all of the plaintiffs. This was also the first time I met *my* hero, Charlie Morgan.

Her head was shaved, and she came up and hugged me. One hug, and I felt like I had known her my entire life. She was such a sweet person. She spoke bravely that night about her cancer, being given months to live, and spending the last moments of her life fighting for the right to leave her wife and daughter with survivor benefits. Even after having given selflessly as a lesbian serving silently under "Don't Ask, Don't Tell," this woman was choosing to spend her last living days fighting for other people's rights. It is profound to watch someone who is dying go out of her way to help others. Seeing the openness of her heart changed my life. So this quickly came to be about Charlie. We wanted to defeat DOMA before she died. This was now a race, and time was not on our side.

SLDN presented all the plaintiffs with the Barry Winchell Award of Courage. Barry Winchell was an army infantry soldier. He started dating someone on his base, and rumors started that he was gay. He got into an altercation with another person, and one of their mutual friends made fun of the guy for letting a "faggot" beat him up. So he took a baseball bat and killed

Winchell in his sleep on July 5, 1999. What was significant was that SLDN used this incident to press for a review of DADT. Winchell's parents (whom we met at the SLDN dinner) also pressed for change to Defense Secretary William Cohen, so in a lot of ways this was what had started much of the discussion around DADT. Here is a written statement from SLDN about Barry Winchell:

> This July marks the 10th anniversary of the murder of PFC Barry Winchell at Fort Campbell in Kentucky. One of the privileges of my job with SLDN is having the honor of meeting and getting to know Barry's parents, Pat and Wally Kutteles—two of the strongest, most genuine and courageous people I know. Each year they come to Washington, D.C. and talk to members of congress about their son's murder in an effort to convince lawmakers why we need to repeal "Don't Ask, Don't Tell." Each year they retell the story of what happened to their son. Each year they relive the horror of what happened to Barry. And each year I marvel at their grace and composure in doing so.

> I had no idea this was coming, but it was an honor to sit there with Barry Winchell's mom and dad at our table. I can't imagine the pain they had gone through, and you could feel all the love for them in the auditorium. It was like they had adopted all of us, thousands of us, in their son's memory. The thing that struck me when I was talking to Barry Winchell's mom was that they still didn't even know if he was gay. The people who killed him suspected him of being gay. I was in awe that his mother and father had embraced the gay community just because their son was slaughtered for this suspicion. They didn't care whether he was or wasn't; they recognized that a human life is a human life and that no one deserves to be treated as their son had been. Barry, even if you were not gay, the gay community honors you and pulls you into its embrace forever.

I was honored to receive this award, and it kept refueling this fire in my heart to make things right. I never wanted another parent to have to go through what Barry's parents had.

That evening we also met Thomas Roberts from MSNBC, who emceed the event. Roberts came out publicly and later legally married his partner. He would also cover my story on several occasions and even interview me on MSNBC.

While we were in Washington DC for the SLDN dinner, the group Freedom to Marry asked Josh and me to film an informal video, sitting and talking in front of a camera. We ended up joking and laughing and just being "us." Not too long ago they released the video they had cut. Oh my God, it was powerful. Sometimes you go through life naturally and without thought. Then later you are a spectator for what has happened to you. As I watched this video, I started to cry. You can see how much Josh and I love each other as we talk. I keep looking at him as he talks about the mortars hitting in Iraq when we were Skyping. And I look into the camera, point to my ring, and say, "I am not taking this off . . . *for anyone*." We were engaging the media like crazy during this time, telling our stories and advocating for change. We were also invited to Logo TV's New, Now, Next Awards. They wanted to do a tribute to servicemembers who were fighting for marriage equality. That night was surreal: we met so many actors and LGBT supporters. We got to meet and hang out with actor Andrew Rannells from the hit show *The New Normal*. We need more gay role models.

One of Josh's coworkers wrote a letter to *The Ellen DeGeneres Show*. She explained how much of an inspiration my story was to her and said that she thought Ellen needed to hear it for herself. I never knew she had written it until we got a call from one of Ellen's production staff. The staff member seemed interested on the phone, but we never received a call back after that. This hurts because someone like Ellen has the power to bring light to real stories of human rights and oppression; I hope that ratings don't get in the way of the important influence she could have on popular opinion. That was a big disappointment, a missed opportunity to tell our story. By this point my story had been covered everywhere from *The Daily Show* to *Rachel Maddow*. It was still very relevant to people, as the 2012 elections were heating up.

So many relationships end when people get deployed. You constantly want affirmation that the person you left behind will wait for you. One of the sweet things Josh did while I was in Iraq to let me know our relationship could weather deployment was to get an arm-sleeve tattoo depicting our story. Our Internet was slow as molasses in Iraq, but Josh and I always attempted to play Worms. When it worked, it was interactive, so we felt like we were right beside each other. His tattoo showed the game, complete with scores by our names (of course he made his team winning) and the Skype symbol to symbolize our life over the last year. I have never been a big tattoo person, but somehow this gave me reassurance of how much he loved me. I mean, what's more comforting than your partner permanently tattooing his entire arm? Get a ring for your finger, or tattoo your entire arm? Once I returned, I did the same in order to also tell our story through art. The only difference between our tattoos is that I placed our marriage date on my arm. I am so proud of him and proud to be with him that I want to show it off to the world. I love this man.

Our first wedding anniversary came quickly. We treated ourselves to some house-renovation projects. My parents sent an anniversary card with money that we used to have a romantic dinner at the same place where we had eaten fondue before I left for Iraq. It was a sweet ending to a story that had started at the same place. We had gone through so much in the past year, but we had made it through even stronger.

Perhaps the best anniversary gift we received that year was from a gentleman named Michael Bedwell. It was a big package that arrived one day while I was at work, addressed to the Snyder-Hill Family. I opened it, not having any idea what it was. Inside was a happy anniversary card from Bedwell, who identified himself as someone who had known Leonard Matlovich. Bedwell sent us the actual *Time* magazine issue that featured Matlovich on the cover. It was surreal, knowing this had come from the friend of a gay rights pioneer. We were honored. What a small world: someone who personally knew one of my heroes had contacted us. Later some of Leonard's family members also became friends of ours on Facebook.

16 The Right to Hyphenate

It was important to me and Josh that we take each other's last names. Until we are no longer denied civil rights, we have to piece our lives together to gain some semblance of equality in terms of being treated as a married couple. We picked a day (and it felt a lot like the day we went to DC for our wedding) to go to the courthouse and get all the papers. It was a process that should have been pretty simple.

We arrived at the probate court, got our paperwork, and sat down to start filling it all out. We noticed a woman who was married (legally) and came in to change her name. It seemed easy for her compared with what we were doing. Josh approached the desk and asked, "How hard it is after getting married to change your name?" The clerk said it was really easy, just a small fee and a couple of signatures. But for us it cost $138 each, and we each had about ten sheets of information to fill out. Then we found out there would be a waiting period and a court date. Regardless of whatever hoops they'd make us jump through, we wanted to do it. We were excited and didn't anticipate we would have any problem, except for the additional cost and missed time at work.

Then the paperwork asked the reason we wanted a name change. My first instinct was to lie, as I had become a professional at trying to hide Josh on all paperwork in the military. But then I relaxed, thinking it was just a routine question. So I wrote, "Because I am legally married to Joshua in the District of Columbia." Josh wrote the same. We even put that we understood the marriage was not recognized in Ohio. When we handed it in, the clerk said, "Wait a minute, I will have to check on this." He came back out and told us we might want to go speak to a magistrate. All of a sudden I felt like some kid who had gotten caught shoplifting and was being dragged to see the store manager. I thought this process was supposed to go smoothly.

We went into the room and were greeted by a woman who seemed uncomfortable, like she had to break bad news to us. The magistrate apologized and told us she didn't want us to waste our money. She said that our request would most likely be denied based on our statement that we were married. She showed us the case that went all the way to the Ohio Supreme Court that would be the reason for the denial of our name change. I was pissed. Josh started to tear up.

"You can lie on your application, and you can put *any* reason," she said, "except something indicating you are doing it for fraud or to avoid bills . . . or gay marriage."

I felt so low. To be compared to someone committing fraud. Talk about second-class citizenship. Screw this. We withdrew our applications. As we started down in the elevator, Josh looked at me, his eyes still watery.

"I still want to apply," he said. "I want to make a stand for my rights."

"I don't want to waste my money in a bigoted state that won't accept my marriage," I said, knowing full well that I couldn't see him this upset and continue to say no. Josh later wrote a blog post about the day:

> We could have written that we don't like our last names and *bam* we're Snyder-Hill. We headed for the elevator, but before we left the building, a realization hit us both. If we didn't apply, if we didn't do this, we would be missing a

chance to at least appeal to a judge about our situation. And if we didn't do this now, then when? We took the elevator back up to the 22nd floor and submitted our applications, unchanged.

We submitted those apps because of the injustice behind this. We need to help people understand what this is, how it truly affects us. Marriage equality will not change anything for the people who are married. What it will do is give dignity to the people who are being denied those same rights. I will not accept shaming ourselves in what already is a degrading and second-class method to take the name of a person I love, a person who has fought for his country, a person who in my eyes can be rivaled by no other. We will not win equality by lying, by giving up because we've been defeated, by sitting at home pouting, or accepting the status quo. We must stand up, speak out and educate every single person who crosses our path.

We went back upstairs. Everyone looked surprised to see us again. The person who had sent us to the magistrate was sitting with her, talking about us. It was like they had no idea what we were about to say or do. We told them they would simply have to deny us our right to get our name changed and that if they did so we would appeal. As we left, I knew we were doing the right thing. They set our court date for June 21, 2012. You can bet we were planning on making a stink. People needed to see what kind of a world we live in when we can't even change our own names. In the meantime a coworker told me she had changed her name (both first and last), and the reason she wrote on the application was that her given name was stupid. It was approved without contest.

Based on what they told us, we were pretty sure we would be denied. But as June 21 approached, we heard from a lot of our supporters how mad our situation made them. We went on television interviews with John Fugelsang on Current TV. We created a Facebook event with all the details of the hearing, in case anyone wanted to come out to support us when the court case was in session. We started getting confirmations from people who wanted to attend and show support, so many that we worried people would be there protesting. We wanted this to be peaceful.

The night before the hearing the local news came to our home to interview us. They were fascinated by the fact that the magistrate had told us to lie. Let me be clear . . . *the magistrate had told us to lie*. She had suggested that we use any reason other than the truth. When you change the truth to something else, you tell a lie. With the news story airing the night before, we knew the probate court would be on alert.

A large group of people showed up, including former congresswoman Mary Jo Kilroy. One of our supporters, Alex, even created a sign with a clever slogan: "2-4-6-8! Let Josh and Steve hyphenate!" We walked into the office on the twenty-second floor, and it was obvious that everyone had been alerted we were coming. (The news said they had tried to contact the probate court for comment on the story the night before.) The guy at the desk was careful and considerate. He was over-the-top conversational, explaining every part of the process. The news was there to follow up on the outcome of the story they had run the night before.

They called us into the courtroom, and I had butterflies in my stomach. What if we were approved? What if they denied us? So many thoughts kept coming. The judge called us up to his bench and started asking our names and why we wanted to change them.

"Because we were married in Washington DC," I said.

"Do you have any credit together? Is the deed on the house in both of your names?"

"No," I said.

"Will changing your names make life more convenient?" he probed.

"No," I said, getting the impression he was trying to get me to change my reason.

What I had told the news reporters was that I had spent the last twenty years lying about who I am, and I wasn't willing to do that anymore. After serving in two wars, defending my country and the rights and civil liberties of its people, I would not alter another damn thing in my life for the convenience of someone else. If my reason for changing my name was that I had married Josh in DC, then damn it, that was my reason. I was not trying to circumvent Ohio law; they asked my reason, and I gave it to them.

As the judge started to speak, we thought we would be denied. Instead, with a news camera pointing at him, he said, "Thank you. I will take this under consideration and put my explanation in a letter to you."

He refused to give his ruling on camera. This is not how such court cases typically go; most people find out the judge's decision on the day of the court appearance. So a camera in the courtroom could alter the outcome of justice? That made no sense. So we waited. We waited for a letter that could deny us in silence, not in front of an audience of people who had no idea how methodically our rights were taken away every day. This was disappointing. The news asked us to keep them updated when the letter arrived. We kept engaging the media to bring attention to this insane situation. The more publicity we drew to it, the more attention and pressure would be put on Ohio.

Time went on, and we received nothing. Finally I emailed the probate court to ask when we could expect the verdict. They responded that the ruling had come out the same day I emailed and that we had been granted our name change. In his ruling the judge cited the earlier case (01-0609, *In re*

Bicknell, 2002-Ohio-3615). The original case had been denied, but the plaintiffs had appealed to the Ohio Supreme Court, which had ruled in their favor. The ruling stated that as long as the plaintiffs didn't use the term *marriage*, they were not trying to circumvent Ohio law. It basically said that they were just fond of each other and that there was no harm in letting them change their names. But as an ironic twist the same court case the magistrate had cited to tell us we would get denied (because it clearly states that the two women were not calling their relationship a marriage) was now used to approve our request. The judge walked through a very detailed explanation of his opinion, stating that we were married but that acknowledging that our marriage wasn't recognized in Ohio did not circumvent Ohio law.

This was cool on so many levels. First, it set a precedent for other people wanting to change their names, citing marriage in another state. But most important, it reinforced the importance of taking a stand for what you believe. On the day we applied for the name change, I felt defeated. I wanted to tear up the application and leave. But something inside of Josh was so enraged that he wanted to fight. Had we torn up our application, we would have been quitters. We not only challenged what that first magistrate said, but we took it to the news, fought publicly, and won.

This victory gave us pause and made us think about Leonard Matlovich. What we felt at this moment was probably how he felt when he won his case. Maybe he was looking down on us in this process. Had he watched Josh and me get married at his grave? Had he watched me get booed on national TV? Such thoughts definitely made us wonder about the afterlife. But beyond metaphysics all this taught me one thing: never quit, and never let someone else limit what you can do. This was an important life lesson for me. I am now Stephen Snyder-Hill, and that's only because we rejected the first opinion we got.

Now I had to adapt to a new identity with a different last name. Normally, changing your name is a pain. But in our case it also involved having to come out over and over again. From credit cards to forms of identification, proving the validity of our new name required showing our marriage certificate, which of course lists two males with different last names. Then we were stuck telling the story all over about how we had been married in DC, but Ohio doesn't recognize our marriage. Then different places had to figure out if they accepted our marriage certificate or not, even though our names had been legally changed. These are examples of things gay people have to go through in states without marriage equality.

Another change I had to make was to order new army uniform nametags and dog tags. When they arrived, I opened the tiny package, and it hit me: sometimes the littlest things have the biggest effect. It was like that moment in a movie when you take a breath and say to yourself, "Holy crap, I love this movie!" To see the name "Snyder-Hill" on my army uniform was one of the proudest moments of my life.

I am still fighting to get Ohio and the federal government to recognize my marriage. But for a moment I put that nametag on my uniform, and it all came together. I am out. Everyone knows about me now. And though no one has to officially recognize my marriage, by God, they will acknowledge my married name—married to another man—on my army uniform. I felt like the first African American who decided to take a sip from the whites-only water fountain and dared someone to say something. I felt like Neil Armstrong: one small step for me but a giant leap for equality.

Josh and I went to a "Welcome Home Warrior" awards ceremony in Cleveland. A lot of the people who were there had not seen me since Iraq, and this was the first time they saw my new nametags. There were no negative reactions, mostly curious gazes at my new name. I wore it proudly. I thought back to

Iraq, when my friend Tims told me, "You will walk out there, with your head high and your shoulders back." And that's just what I did that day in Cleveland.

People don't realize the thoughts that go through a gay person's head regarding something as simple as a name change. I can't count the number of times I have seen soldiers get married and get a new last name—or get divorced and revert back. But for me this was so much more. Twenty years of struggling and making up stories and lying, all pushed to the curb along with "Don't Ask, Don't Tell."

When I went up on stage to be presented with my award, my colonel looked at my uniform and smiled. "Name change, I see!" he said. I will never know if that was a little mini-congratulations, but it felt like it.

This even caused things to happen at my civilian job. A woman at my place of work recently called me upon seeing my hyphenated last name to say she didn't know I was married. I assumed she had seen all the media about me, so when she said her son had hyphenated his name too, I thought she was telling me her son was gay. Then as she continued to talk, it was clear that her son and his wife had hyphenated their last names. She mentioned that name changes are pretty easy because of the marriage certificate process. So I went for it and said, "Oh, but my marriage is not recognized in Ohio because I am married to a man." There was silence on the other end of the line. I think she felt a little uncomfortable, but I don't think it was because she feels negatively about gay people. I just think that when you put yourself out there, sometimes it's awkward. But for the first time in my life I felt like it was okay for someone else to be a little uncomfortable, because I had felt that way my entire life. I didn't do it to be mean; I just wanted to be upfront with her. The only way to provoke change is to tell your story.

Josh had the same thing happen at his work. His boss said, "You know, I have never asked you what your wife's name was."

A gay guy who works with Josh was there at the time, so he just laughed and said, "Awkward." Josh then explained it all to his boss, who felt bad for assuming. But it's not his boss's fault. It's because gay people learn to protect ourselves so much by changing all of our pronouns to neutral words that we just get used to it. Josh had known his boss for a while and always talked about me in a neutral way.

The name change is one way we've been outing ourselves to friends and strangers alike, but there are other ways too. Josh and I were out of town at a hotel pool recently for an event we spoke at, and a woman playing with her son took notice of my dog tags around Josh's neck. He had started wearing them when I left for Iraq, and much like my mom's light in the window, he had decided never to take them off. To this day he still wears them, and he even wanted to keep one with my old last name because those are the ones he wore for a year. The woman told us she was retired military and asked Josh if he was in the military. He said, "No, they're his," pointing to me. She didn't have much to say in response, so we left it at that. People do not realize that gay people are forced to come out every day. And some people feel like we are throwing it in their faces that we are gay, when we are simply trying to live our lives and not lie or hide from anyone anymore.

The same thing happened to us at the airport. One of the TSA guys thanked Josh for his service, and again Josh pointed to me. He saw my dogtags and our tattoos. The guy said, "Is that your brother?" Josh just kind of shrugged. These are the moments I want to capture in this book because people do not realize that every day of your life as a gay person, you have to make a decision to either make someone uncomfortable or just let it go. For years I wanted to protect everyone else. It is only now that I am starting to realize I am not protecting anyone; I am harming myself. Josh and I have started making a conscious effort to use these opportunities to just be honest. Silence = Death.

17 Presidential Momentum

In May 2012 Joe Biden was asked his opinion on gay marriage. He basically said that he has no problem with it. The media went crazy! Then rumors started to percolate that President Obama would come out in support of gay marriage. How important was this? Of course, without legislation to support our rights, it was just his opinion. But any time a political figure publicly supports marriage equality, it is a wonderful step in the right direction. And sure enough, President Obama made such a public statement during an ABC interview. It was an awesome day and a wonderful feeling. I felt like this was the America I had been fighting for.

We went to a party that night to celebrate the president's announcement. A grassroots media reporter interviewed me about my thoughts on the endorsement. I mentioned how proud it made me to have Obama as my president. There were people who said that the president supported me as a political move. My response is that he didn't know how people would react, so even if it was politically motivated, it might have had a negative effect. For him to go out on a limb to lobby for civil rights for LGBT people just before an election made a statement about the kind of man he was. President Obama was living the words he used against the Republican candidates: he was standing up for LGBT men and women even when it wasn't politically convenient. That reaffirmed my pride at being deployed under this historical president. The next thing that happened was that

I was invited onto the *Ed Schultz Show*, opposite Clay Aiken, to talk about the president's endorsement. This was not the first time I had been engaged by the media: I had been on *Hardball with Chris Matthews* and many other shows. But I had to be careful with my words, since they were asking me directly about political candidates and the president. I think I did a good job. They played Mitt Romney's response to the booing (he doesn't make it a practice to scold the audience) and then asked me what I thought of it. I answered truthfully by ignoring Romney's response and instead highlighting how proud I was to be deployed under a president who stood up for me when it would have been just as easy not to speak out.

Everything I have fought for in the army for over twenty years is meant to ensure that the most qualified candidate—regardless of skin color—has the opportunity to become president of the United States. This includes allowing people who love each other to marry and have the same rights as other people in our free country. This is *everything* America is about. I focused on this and ignored Mitt Romney trying to cover for the missed opportunity to do what was right.

SLDN contacted me a month later to appear on *The War Room*, a show on Al Gore's network, Current TV. The host, John Fugelsang, told me that out of all the people he wanted to have on the show, I was the one he most wanted to talk to. But as luck would have it, my earpiece kept popping out. That was my first moment in the media spotlight where everything seemed to go wrong as I was talking. It is amazing how one singular distraction while you are on live TV can mess up your thought process. We focused mostly on our name change, and it all turned out okay in the end. It's just one of those moments I'd change if I could.

In all of our travels on the media circuit Josh and I started making new contacts, and our friend requests started lighting up on Facebook. We started talking to a woman from Ithaca,

New York, named Rachel Hockett. She had friended Josh on Facebook while I was in Iraq, and she became our fan and a supporter. Rachel was the director of the Homecoming Players, a group of actors she had assembled from several different theater companies. They won the chance to perform a reading of Dustin Lance Black's play 8, based on the Proposition 8 trials in California. Proceeds from their performance of the play would go toward the fight for marriage equality. In August 2012 Rachel invited Josh and me to be guests of honor at the performance, along with Ithaca's mayor. At the time we didn't know much about the play, other than it was about the court case and had been written by the guy who also wrote *Milk* and that a lot of famous actors had been involved in performing the play in other states.

Once we arrived in Ithaca, we met up with Rachel and her roommate, Arthur, and knew immediately that we had found new friends for life. They were so supportive of us and of our activism. The people of Ithaca were all so warm toward us: this was the first time we actually felt like mini-celebrities. I assumed the auditorium would be set up for a play, but when we entered, we saw chairs arranged in courtroom style, complete with water bottles. Then Rachel came out and introduced the production, and it all started to make sense. The actors were reading the actual transcripts of the case: how cool!

The Proposition 8 court case was such bullshit that Dustin Lance Black had decided the public had a right to know the extent of the bigotry behind it. So he took the transcripts of the case and let those words tell the story of how crazy our court system can be. During the play, for example, the judge actually asks the lawyer how he knows gay marriage will damage the sanctity of straight marriage. The lawyer's response is, "It's on the Internet." Those words made the hair on the back of my neck stand up! Black added only a small amount of dialogue to the play to develop the characters for the audience, and his approach was effective. Josh cried at one point, when the mother explains to her son why they have to be in court defending themselves.

Then I realized how important this play really is. Our rights are being determined in court by people who present evidence that's based not on fact, but on bias, hate, and flat-out lies. And, to boot, the American people are being shielded from the truth because the transcripts of this court case were not released, and the media was not allowed to cover it. This is the America I believe in and fight for?

The actors did such a good job; even though it was a reading, they read with emotion and power! As I watched those players, I felt like they were acting out our lives. Afterward they invited Josh and me on stage along with the mayor of Ithaca. We all spoke, and I told them that their work had really hit home. I talked about our real-life case with SLDN, and the audience response was overwhelming. When Josh and I got home, we discovered that the Homecoming Players had fallen a little more than five hundred dollars short of their eight-thousand-dollar fundraising goal for marriage equality. Without hesitation Josh and I donated exactly what they needed. It was like the last piece of perfection in this awesome performance.

With every new event we attend and every new person we meet, I am amazed at the conviction so many people have of the importance of "righting" the "civil wrongs" that persist in this country. Wonderful experiences like our trip to Ithaca and my television interviews give me the strength to keep my cool when I see bigotry, the flip side of all this positivity. Recently Josh and I were taking our dogs for a walk at home in Columbus. We weren't dressed in anything particularly eye catching or acting affectionate; we were just two guys walking dogs. All of a sudden a van zoomed by, and someone shouted, "Faggots!" I asked Josh, "Did they just call us faggots? In 2012? Who does that? Were they in high school?" Times like these reminded me that you might live in a bubble where you think everyone supports you, and then along comes someone with a needle. Sometimes I cannot believe people have so much hatred inside themselves.

About the same time one of my friends posted on Facebook that his car had been keyed with the word *faggot*. It was like someone was trying to remind me not to forget that the world we live in can still be cruel. But this realization just made me want to fight harder. I really do believe those studies that say that the most homophobic people are actually closeted people trying to overcompensate to hide their identity.

Josh's outlet for dealing with antigay experiences is blogging, which he has been doing with increased frequency. Sometimes to convey what bigotry really means, you have to get creative with your use of metaphor. That's how you reach people. Josh is particularly good at this and has written so many things that move me. Here are a few examples:

2004 FAILURE
Imagine being in the hottest club in the biggest city of your dreams. People are dancing, some moving in a rhythm you wish you could, others clumsily, and then of course there's you, with your own private rain dance.

The music intensifies, people seem energized, some mixed track is about to blend into the hottest song of the year, and you close your eyes and wait for the beat. The song begins and you're dancing, probably even singing out loud knowing the music will drown out your off-key octaves. Finally you open your eyes. The crowd of hundreds that was moving to a unified beat has suddenly changed; every other person is just standing and gawking. Suddenly the song doesn't feel so right, you don't even feel the beat anymore, all you notice is hundreds of people standing, doing nothing. Then without warning you notice you're no longer dancing.

Early November in 2004, overnight America lost the chance of marriage equality in 23 states. A battle struck out over "traditional marriage," a battle trying to define what it was and more importantly what it was not. That year, when LGBT rights had probably not seen injustice the likes of the days of Harvey Milk, our community failed.

In 2004 a super majority within our very own community did not vote. We gave our opposing side a 12-point bump. You might say that 60% of the LGBT community would only equal 6% of the entire population. You're right, but if 6% does not vote for our side, then we don't neutralize 6% of the opposing side's vote. Now suddenly bigotry gains by 12%.

So this is how we failed. We didn't even find our own unified voice; less than half of us danced.

Activism is a contact sport. No, it's not physical, but your emotion will be bruised. The LGBT is a minority, but understand that the only reason people fear and shun us is because they have been taught to do so; they have been taught to fear what they don't understand. The one most organic thing we all understand is love; connect with people on that level and the fear subsides. 2012 cannot be a repeat of 2004; we cannot afford to fall backward after making so much progress. Love is the easiest thing to understand but fear and inaction will bring out the worst in all of us.

YOUR VOTE IS NOT ENOUGH

If there is one thing I have learned, it's that my vote is a final effort of what must be a greater cause. I do believe that every vote counts, but if we don't have open dialogue, it is all for naught.

I have had the amazing privilege of speaking in front of over 3,000 people. Do you know how many people I can say for sure I have convinced to vote? Ten, I can say with great pride and conviction that I have seen the light switch click, the OMG moment cross a person's mind and a point of view change. I am proud of this, but I can say it with 100% confidence for only those ten people.

Take the time and start to talk to your friends. You may think they are going to vote, and you may think they are helping people understand our rights are being denied, but the truth is that you really don't know until you ask. As politically active as I am, I have come to realize that I have close friends who were not taking it seriously, who were not going to vote.

Our rights, our lives are being put in the hands of a majority of people who do not understand what it's like to be us. I have awesome news, though: a majority of people are good; a majority of people will listen to reason. When you have someone stand in your shoes, when you make them think of how it would feel to have their husband or wife be shamed or treated as less, when you make them think of how much they love their children, the fear that comes from not understanding melts away and the passion for love overrides.

When I walk into the voting booth this November I will imagine the line of people I have created. I will think of the people who were not going to vote and the people who were going to vote against my rights but changed their minds. I will think of all the conversations that may have felt repetitive, that may have been less fun than drinking, or joking, or even sleeping. I will smile and know that I have gone far beyond being just one vote; I have been one voice that has influenced many.

THE LOVE STORY OF JESSICA AND STEVE

Early in the summer of 2010, a young professional named Jessica met a man named Steve. They quickly realized they were soul mates who, from that point forward, would be inseparable. Steve was in the Army. One evening at dinner, Steve posed the question, "What would you do if I was deployed?" Jessica looked him in the eyes and said, "I would wait for you." They both wiped tears from their eyes and sighed with relief.

Late September Jessica heard Steve come home and start walking up the stairs. She peeked around the corner down the hall, and as she was about to say hello, she saw that Steve was crying. "We have to talk," he mouthed, and Jessica's heart dropped. Steve was going to Iraq; the romantic dinner promise made months ago was now a reality.

Their families had grown close, both parents claiming a new child, making promises to help each other through the next year. Within a month Steve was being driven to base by four parents now instead of two. Jessica and Steve would have one final goodbye before he left for Iraq. They would spend their first Thanksgiving in Seattle, alone. "You're my wife after this," Steve whispered. She nodded; she already knew that.

Steve and Jessica spent some of their first holidays via Skype over the next year, Christmas, Easter, and Valentine's Day to name a few. While unnatural at first, chatting through a grainy video link gradually became something they both looked forward to. In the middle of conversation one morning, an odd sound rang in the background. Jessica's brain tried to register the noise, and the line disconnected. Jessica sat confused, she felt as if she was in slow motion and the world was hurling past her. Steve's words were still processing: "I have to go, that was a mortar."

Two hours passed before the bubbly Skype sound would finally ring in. Jessica had not moved from that spot since she last heard Steve's voice. A mortar had landed only a few yards shy of where he slept. Steve was now exhausted, so he blew her his regular kiss goodnight. The screen went dark, and Jessica cried herself to sleep.

Steve was coming home for R&R and the excitement was overwhelming. He looked into her eyes and said, "I'd marry you tomorrow." The following Monday, they would get married at a private ceremony. Steve would return to Iraq just a few short days later. The next six months felt long for them both. Another mortar would disconnect the two for hours, Jessica waiting and hoping the next call would be Steve. In the end Steve would return home, and the two would live life the way they knew best. Steve was a hero in Jessica's eyes and truly in the world's.

What if there was a change to this story, this real story? What if Jessica was actually Joshua? Does it make the love less real? Does it make the dedication, the challenges, and the victories less commendable? And if it does change because of a name, does it say anything about the couple, or more about the person reading this?

WHEN A STICKER IS JUST A STICKER

Please understand that often while I know my blogs come across as angry and seem to be slamming the LGBT community, there is good intent. The reason I feel I can be so critical, is honestly because I think I have been on the side I am ridiculing. That's hard for me to admit, but I honestly know I could have been a true activist sooner.

I drive down the road regularly and notice them, our little pride stickers. Maybe it's HRC, or a rainbow stripe, maybe it's a cute little family portrait of stick figures like I have on my car, with two guys holding hands, two dogs and a cat. Whatever it is, a number of the LGBT members out there sport some little banner showing their pride. My question is, so what? Do you really think you're a proponent for change?

Steve and I were talking the other day about some friends who take advantage of the rights they have been afforded. They slap some sticker on their bumper and feel they are paying homage to a great cause. In all honesty they are enjoying the benefits of people fighting a battle that is not over.

I've been trying to learn the history of our LGBT community. I've started to gain a great respect and realized we have
to finish this battle and do right by the people who fought
before us. The gay community has become complacent; we
play on apps like Grindr, we dance in our nightclubs, and we
strut our stuff at Pride. We forget that 30 years ago all this
could have gotten us arrested, beaten or killed.

Now I know some you think I speak blasphemy and that
the mere enjoyment of these liberties is celebrating our
successes. That thought process is flawed and as blind and
ignorant as the people who are seeking to take our rights
away. This is *not* what Harvey Milk, Leonard Matlovich, and
the likes were fighting for. They were not fighting for us to
become complacent with a second-class position, to not be
granted the same benefits as other married couples, families,
or workers. They fought for the respect we deserve and do
not yet have.

In many states we can't get benefits, we can't adopt, we
can't visit our dying spouse, we can't marry. Even if we can
marry in some states, it means nothing on a federal level.
We pay higher taxes, higher insurance premiums, and can
get fired simply for who we love. It's even politically OK to
equate us to pedophiles and those who practice bestiality.

If one LGBT member is suffering from injustice, we are all
suffering. If you don't realize this, if you don't feel moved to
get up and start being a true activist, then you are as much a
part of the problem. Our battle is not over. This should not
dishearten us; this should strengthen us.

A path has been set by some amazing leaders of our past.
We are moving forward but it's not time to slow down; it's
time to scream at the top of our lungs, to fight for our community and look far beyond ourselves. Be more than that
sticker. Be a part of a history that makes that sticker obsolete,
a sign of what used to be a division in this great country.

I think that the rally in Cleveland was the moment Josh really started thinking about how to be an activist. He kept bringing up the president's "evolving" status on gay marriage. So he decided to start a new website that would be called "Marriage Evolved." At first the concept was to try to get people to protest DOMA and hold their marriages only in states that had true marriage equality. But he realized that this would never gain traction quickly enough. So he worked on the logo and the site, eventually releasing it to a select group of people.

The premise was simple: send in a video and talk about what "Marriage Evolved" means to you. He was patterning his campaign on the "It Gets Better" project, started by Dan Savage to urge gay teens to be proud of who they are and not believe the hurtful messages of bullies. He started getting lots of videos. One was really cute—a little girl who talked about how she just couldn't believe than in 2012 people were opposed to people marrying who they loved.

The video I submitted was based on the opening lyrics of the Pink Floyd song "Keep Talking." I said that to me "Marriage Evolved" means using your voice. The only thing that makes us different from animals is our ability to articulate our thoughts. We need to use this power now to fight for our rights and to help public sentiment evolve just as a species would. I ended by saying sometimes evolution has to be provoked by revolution.

Marriage equality is such a hot-button issue that even groups on the same side can't agree on how to move progress forward. There was a group of people representing the "Freedom to Marry" petition to repeal the 2004 DOMA that had been voted on in Ohio. Then there were other LGBT groups that thought more time and planning had to be put into trying to get this initiative on the ballot.

Josh and I stayed neutral; our only course was to tell our story. I think that is the most powerful thing you can do. That is why deep down in my heart I kept thinking of Rosa Parks.

What if she had kept saying, "Maybe I should wait for another time"? What if she had not spoken up that day? Where would we be today?

One thing that makes me furious is that, especially today, people use gay rights as talking points for political agendas. But these are our lives. These policies affect real people. This is no game. But it is treated as such. Romney used his anti-gay-marriage stance to win conservative votes, and President Obama probably won over some liberal voters. I hope people realize that we are real people and not some strategy to get into office.

18 One Year of Freedom

On September 20, 2012, I stared at Josh as he pressed my shirt in a New York City hotel room, reflecting on everything that had happened over the past year—and over the past twenty years. All of it came full circle on this night. One year ago I had been breathing in the dusty air of Iraq. I remembered taking a deep inhalation of sand and soot, then exhaling every last drop of fear that remained in my grateful lungs the day the repeal of "Don't Ask, Don't Tell" was made official. That one legislative action changed my life in so many ways. This was going to be a big night.

SLDN had arranged a celebration of the one-year anniversary of the "Don't Ask, Don't Tell" repeal. We didn't want to be late, so instead of taking the subway we hailed a cab. Once we arrived, Zeke Stokes, the communications director of SLDN, escorted us into a special holding area. Headlining the event would be an address by Admiral Mike Mullen, who had been instrumental in ushering the repeal through Congress. Barbara Walters would be the emcee.

Josh and I waited in line at the red carpet. I had never had a red carpet experience before; I had never thought myself important enough to need one (and still do not). Zeke called us forward and introduced me as the soldier who was booed in the GOP debates and Josh as my husband. The flashes started flying. People started yelling, "Over here, please." For a moment I felt like I was going to have a seizure. The other plaintiffs from our lawsuit were also part of the paparazzi moment on the red carpet.

Barbara Walters came out and addressed the crowd, to thunderous applause. We never got to talk to her in person, but she was a great emcee. At one point in her talk she mentioned that never again would servicemembers have to hide to serve their country. I lost it and screamed out in excitement. It was like twenty years of bottled-up, suppressed feeling just had to escape. She paused and looked directly at me in the front row. She smiled and said, "Exactly," then yelled out a "woo-woooo." She laughed and said, "I didn't do it quite as well as him, everybody," and the audience screamed. The energy was incredible.

Across the crowd we spotted Randy Jones from the Village People. You couldn't miss him; he was dressed up as a cowboy in a ten-gallon hat. Josh and I spent some time talking to him. Josh said something about being a bit of a ham. Randy replied, "Well, you know I am cheese, and you know that ham goes with cheese." Randy's husband was more of the quiet type. He rolled his eyes a lot, so you knew he must be used to Randy's colorful comments. I was excited to tell him my dog's name was Macho and that every time I heard the Village People "Macho Man" song, I sang it to my dog.

That night we also met one of my personal heroes, Patrick Murphy, the U.S. representative from Pennsylvania who had introduced the bill to repeal "Don't Ask, Don't Tell." The HBO film *The Strange History of Don't Ask, Don't Tell* mentions Representative Murphy, a straight army veteran who stood up for us, and I remember thinking what a hero this guy was. I introduced myself, and he smiled and said, "When I saw you on TV, you inspired me to start working out." Then he said, "Ironically enough, I worked out with Paul Ryan for a bit." I wasn't sure if he was joking or not, but it was funny. It was an amazing opportunity to thank him for everything he had done, the person who had introduced the legislation that gave me the freedom I had fought so hard for.

We kept walking around meeting people, including a woman

named Tracey, the wife of Brigadier General Tammy Smith, the first openly gay general officer to come out in the military after the repeal of "Don't Ask, Don't Tell." Brigadier General Smith had sent me a personal note on army stationery when I received my promotion from captain to major. She knew of the booing incident, and she congratulated me on my promotion and encouraged me to lead by example. She was not there, but at least I was able to talk to her wife that night. They are both inspirational people.

Probably one of the most significant events of the evening was my introduction to Rachel Maddow. When I was in Iraq, they showed MSNBC on the Armed Forces Network. I always watched Rachel whenever I had the chance. She has always been an icon to me because she's witty and can deliver a point with a precision that no one else can come close to. She has talked about my story on her show several times, so I felt like she already knew a lot about me. Nervous as could be, I shook her hand and introduced myself as the booed soldier. She smiled and then shook Josh's hand. She didn't seem to react to me at all, which I thought was odd, especially since she was so passionate about me on her show. Later someone told her who I was, and she told Josh, "Your husband needs to enunciate better because I thought he said the *boot soldier*; I didn't know if that was some weird fetish or something." She is even witty in person.

We talked for a while, and I explained more of my story to her. I mentioned the conservative sergeant in my unit whom I wanted her to mention on her show as her number-one fan. I later sent him an email with all of our pictures as a souvenir for his Rush Limbaugh collection. I also told Rachel that I would never forget the way her voice sounded when she said on her show, "They actually *booed* a U.S. servicemember serving his country . . . in Iraq." You could hear her voice shake as she said this. It was chilling. She replied, "It fucking pissed me off." It was so cool to thank her in person for her support.

There were many unforgettable moments throughout this evening, like crossing paths with celebrities and influential people. But for me nothing compared with being able to meet Admiral Mike Mullen. SLDN had created an extremely strategic campaign to get DADT repealed, and Representative Murphy had introduced it. People had testified, and President Obama ultimately had to finally sign the bill. If it weren't for all of these people, I would still be forced to hide pictures in my own home and lie about who I am. Everyone involved was instrumental, but it was really up to Admiral Mullen to put his neck on the line and give his opinion on whether repealing DADT would harm the readiness of the armed forces. He was the voice of the military on whether we should accept this repeal, and as he was about to testify, you could have heard a pin drop in the room.

For a moment I thought again about *The Strange History of Don't Ask, Don't Tell*. In addition to telling the story of heroes like Admiral Mullen and Representative Murphy, it showcases all the opposition at the time from people like John McCain. But recently I heard an interview that McCain did after the GOP debate, and he actually defended me, stating that the Republican candidates should have spoken up in response to the booing. Considering how much he was opposed gay people being in the military, I wondered whether my story had changed his mind. He went from testifying against repealing DADT to being enraged that no one had defended a gay soldier in Iraq. Maybe he just needed to see blatant discrimination against someone who was serving his country to know what was right. Even if we differ in our political views, I respect him for his service to his country. When you wear a uniform, you earn a badge of respect, and it is easier for me to listen to his opinion about the armed forces than the opinion of someone who has never worn the uniform.

There was a VIP reception that night where we could mingle with some of the headliners of the evening. I looked around the room, and there stood Admiral Mullen. People say how much soldiers sacrifice for other people, but I just stared at him, thinking about how much he had sacrificed for me. Admiral Mullen had a lot to lose. Of course he had tons of studies, and he had examples of other countries that have not had an issue with gay people serving, and he knew gay people have always been in the military, but at the end of the day he had to face Congress and the American people and testify.

That night I had such butterflies in my stomach. Even with everything I had been through, and all the people I had met, he was the most important person for me to try to talk to. It was so important for me to be able to thank him. It was very busy at the reception, and there were lots of people waiting to shake his hand. At one point I actually thought I had blown my chance because I wasn't being aggressive enough. Josh, who later told me he had never seen me so nervous before, stood next to me as I waited. I am usually confident, never shy about meeting someone. Tonight was different; I was like a kid. I had a very important mission, and it had to be executed just right.

I walked up and looked into his eyes. I reached out my hand, and he shook it. I told him that I was the soldier who had been booed during the GOP debates last year. He closed his eyes and lowered his head in regret. You could tell this man was sincere. He apologized to me in silence. Then it was my turn to be sincere. I tried my best to convey to him what this entire book sums up. I told him how deeply grateful I am for what he had done for me and for all gay soldiers serving their country. Secrecy and injustice had consumed me for twenty years, leading up to me exposing myself to the world by asking my question on September 22, 2011. I am free, I am allowed to serve the country I love, and I can be who I am without being discharged because I happen to love a man. I owed it all to this man and to President Obama for his support.

It was full circle: twenty years of living a lie, two deployments, one GOP debate, tons of activism, and a media maelstrom. Now

I had the chance to shake the hand of the man who had really made it all possible. Admiral Mullen handed me a coin from the Joint Chiefs of Staff. I framed it, along with a picture of me shaking his hand. I will treasure that picture forever. It hangs on the wall right beside a picture of Josh and me, both pictures that I will never again have to pull off of my wall in fear.

Despite this wonderful celebration of an important victory we still had a long way to go.

That reality came down like an atomic bomb. A few months after the DADT anniversary party I received word one morning that Charlie Morgan had died. It was like a bulldozer had ripped out my insides; it just didn't feel real. I felt like I had lost a family member. They kept saying this was going to happen, and she even said the same thing, but I didn't believe it. We had seen her so much over the last year, and she had texted Josh these cute messages only a couple of weeks ago. To lose someone you love is very hard, but this woman loved everyone. She spent her dying days fighting for other servicemembers. She was a selfless hero, and losing her was devastating. She was a leader, and she inspired me to be a better person. She left behind a wonderful wife, Karen, and their child, Casey. I would dare any human being to look me in the eye and say this family doesn't deserve equality. But sure enough: her wife had no more rights after her death than a friend would have. Shortly after her death the Pentagon released a statement saying they would extend additional benefits (like ID cards) to same-sex military spouses. Charlie didn't live long enough to hear that, and it kills me to this day.

19 All Aboard the C-BUS of Love

What's unique about Josh and me as a couple is that I am the fire and he is the fuel. Back when I was deployed to Iraq in 2010, Josh started several of his own activism initiatives. The first was a website called "Don't Say H8," which was a twist on the Tennessee SB 49 bill outlawing the use of the word *gay* in school. Josh did everything grassroots style, right down to filming several public service announcements with his closest friends and releasing them on the Internet. George Takei was his big inspiration at the time, releasing his own public service announcement about the bill (more on that later). Josh would update me over Skype on what the dontsayh8.com team was doing and what was next in the pipeline. He even had me film little messages from Iraq and include them in the commercials.

I wonder if much of Josh's fuel came from missing a significant part of his life (me) while I was on deployment. When a major upset like this takes place, people often try to cope by finding things that interest them and keep them occupied. Josh started using all of his time coming up with new ideas for fighting inequality. Another one of the ideas he pitched to me was a push to take weddings out of states that didn't have marriage equality.

"Imagine the amount of money people spend on weddings," he said, "and what a huge statement it would be for people to start leaving their home state to be married."

I thought this was way too idealistic. I countered that no

one I knew (even an LGBT advocate) would be willing to take something so sacred to them and uproot it just to make a statement. I always hated offering Josh a dissenting opinion because I could just hear the disappointment in his voice. He has such a great heart, and it all comes from such a sincere place, but sometimes we're very different when it comes to what we think is achievable. I think back to Randy's words: I am the ham, and Josh is the cheese!

Thank goodness for his ability to dream, though, since I would never have thought some of the stuff we do is possible. His idea quickly transformed from a focus on wedding ceremonies to "Marriage Evolved." As people started to sign up and submit their PSAs, Josh immediately created a Facebook group, which exploded to more than twenty thousand members in a short time. Josh asked me for a logo, and I came up with a graphically intertwined M and E that we started plastering all over everything. Next Josh approached me with a compromise: What if we transported a bunch of people to DC to be married? He enlisted his friends Stephanie and Brett, who attended our first meeting about the subject in our dining room in December 2012. While everyone else was thinking about Christmas and holiday shopping, we were at a drawing board making a plan for marriage equality. Josh proposed renting a bus to carry all the couples to DC, and soon our project was branded with the name "C-BUS of Love" (C for Columbus).

Josh has excellent delegation and project-management skills, so he started collecting volunteers and tasking out projects. Brett's job was to negotiate with the bus companies, Stephanie's job was to check the lodging, and mine was to create the logo and promotional material. We started enlisting more help— Rob, Flo, James, and many others. After many meetings we finally came up with an estimate of $495 per couple. We figured this was reasonable, since Josh and I alone had spent a couple hundred dollars on our marriage license and officiant. We knew right away we wanted Tiffany Newman, the woman who had married us, to perform the weddings.

The C-BUS of Love launch date was on Valentine's Day, February 14, 2013. We blasted the event all over Facebook and the "Marriage Evolved" website. Responses were a little slow at first, so we chose a cutoff date to abandon the project if we couldn't get at least twenty-five couples. There were conference calls after conference calls. It was nerve-racking at times because we were past the point of no return. We had couples drop out (from fear of losing their jobs) and couples who couldn't raise the money, even though they said they wanted to go. As we quickly approached our twenty-fifth couple, interest suddenly exploded, so much so that Josh proposed the idea of a second bus. This is why I love this man. It was like we were on the last flight out of a disaster zone, and he didn't want to leave a single soul behind, no matter how practical the rescue mission.

Once we hit our maximum number of couples, we started doing radio spots and asking local businesses to donate goods and services. Josh's eyes lit up the moment he had an epiphany about where the weddings should take place. "The Supreme Court!" he yelled. Once again I thought there was no way we could do this. But he started making calls and discovered that the steps were off-limits, but the public space was allowed. I was so skeptical that I thought for sure we would arrive and get arrested. What made me even more nervous was that DOMA was supposed to be decided and our lawsuit was coming to a head, all at the same time. This was our movie, and the plot was unfolding. Josh promised me he had talked to a security guard, and we would be okay as long as we stayed in a public space.

In the midst of C-BUS planning we received a call from Karla Rothan, the director of Stonewall Union in Columbus. She told us that Josh and I exemplified the theme of this year's Columbus pride parade, "Pride Changes Lives." She then asked if we would consider being the parade's grand marshals. Sometimes you don't realize how much of your life you have devoted to a cause until someone thanks you for it. We proudly accepted, but we couldn't miss a beat; we couldn't let this or anything else slow us down.

Once all the money and donations for the C-BUS wedding started rolling in, we got some bad news. Even with all of the couples paid in full, we were about four thousand dollars short. One of the big snafus was that the bus company was charging us for two days instead of one. As the budget people Stephanie and I started cutting stuff out. Josh was like a little kid getting his toys taken away; he was not having any part of it. He kept giving his classic optimistic viewpoint that it would work out. "I promise," he'd say. He didn't want the experience to be any less than fabulous for his new family of couples, no matter the cost.

We enlisted the help of a local drag queen, Nina West, to help raise money. We also engaged gay-friendly businesses aggressively to get more donations. Nina, a great person who does a lot of LGBT charity work, agreed to do a show, and Josh and I agreed to "perform" to boost attendance. Josh and two other guys decided to do a number, which they practiced over and over again for weeks. I would sing.

Nina introduced me, and I spoke briefly. I asked people to reach deep in their pockets to make this a reality. My song came on, and once I started singing, Nina and another drag queen came out and ripped off my shirt. I was pretty shy and not prepared for that, but the dollar bills started flying.

At one point I looked over at a drag queen who was examining himself in the mirror, as though he were rehearsing to make sure every line was right and every movement was perfect. I was so filled with emotion that I ran out on stage and grabbed the microphone from Nina.

"I feel ashamed that I didn't mention this earlier, but I want to most of all thank all of these drag queens from the bottom of my heart. They are out here donating their time for you tonight," I said.

I thought about that guy in the mirror, who tried to put on the best performance he could . . . for free. He didn't skimp on anything. I thought about how much time, makeup, rehearsing, and everything else goes into performing. I thought about how 99 percent of people would just give the minimum to check off the "I helped" box, but not these people.

"You know this all started with the Stonewall riots years ago," I continued. "Drag queens were out fighting for you then, and they still are up here fighting for you today!"

This drew big applause and was a neck-hair-raising experience, at least for me. We were hoping to raise two thousand dollars, but when all was said and done, we raised every bit of our four thousand dollars. It was like a miracle. We owe a lot to the owner of the club, Rajesh, and all of his employees that night.

The couples going on the bus had quickly become great friends on Facebook. They were such a lively, chatty group. We decided to meet with them before the trip and invited everyone to dinner. Reality dawned on me once I saw them in person: these were human beings with emotions and children, who were so excited to have a chance at equality. I looked silently over at Josh; I never told him how proud I was of him that night. It was very emotional for us watching them bond with each other. We put the finishing touches on our plans, right down to which movies we would bring on the bus (at the couples' request).

The morning of the trip we had to get up at 3 a.m. My parents had driven down the night before to help us load everything into the car and go meet the bus. We had met many of the couples in person previously, but not all. We loaded up the bus (one entire compartment was dedicated to wedding dresses) and started the long trip. Most of us slept, but some people were wired from excitement. We arrived in DC around 1 p.m. and stopped at a rest area so everyone could get dressed and primped. Zeke Stokes, and Allyson Robinson, the director of SLDN, met the couples as they changed. They presented the couples with gifts and some words of encouragement. Some of the brides had a pit crew of family who were giving them bridal makeovers. It was an amazing sight.

We loaded back on the bus and headed for the Supreme Court. The police wouldn't let the bus park in front to unload the couples, so we had to circle around and unload a block away. Tiffany was waiting as we lined up the couples. The police and guards all watched as these twenty-five beautiful couples were married. There was a big cheer when she pronounced them all married. Tons of onlookers were watching.

Out of the corner of my eye I saw one of the guards approaching us. I was terrified. This is it, I thought, sure that we were probably in trouble. It turns out he was so moved by watching the weddings that he had an idea.

"You can't come up on the Supreme Court steps as a group," he said, "but by God, nothing can stop each of the couples walking through as individuals."

Josh instantly started crying. The couples quickly lined up (as a group anyway) and were individually escorted into the Supreme Court building. This was all happening right before the biggest court case for the LGBT community would be decided inside that very building. They were permitted to walk, hand in hand, down the front steps as we announced their names. Each one of them kissed and posed for a picture to be taken by the wedding photographer we had hired to immortalize the trip.

This was one of the most poetic moments I have ever seen. I wanted to jump in and join them, but something in my gut stopped me. This was *their* day, and when I thought back to my wedding day, I realized it was *our* special moment, our special story. This was their turn, so Josh and I watched in amazement.

We loaded back up the bus and headed to a restaurant where the couples had their first dance. Jacob, a chef from Florida, had driven all the way up to bring us gourmet cupcakes with brides and grooms on them. Everything came together like a dream. The couples all received their marriage certificates and were so emotional, instantly posting them to Facebook and changing their relationship status. We had 189 years of commitment on the bus that night. We were so exhausted yet so fulfilled: we had done it!

We made it home by 3 a.m. and hit the sack because we had to lead the pride parade in just a few hours.

20 Chariots and Superheroes

All of the C-BUS couples spent their first night married in a hotel in downtown Columbus. Josh and I met them, along with my parents, on the morning of the "Pride Changes Lives" parade. This would be my parents' first pride march. The float, designed especially for us, was poised at the starting line like a grand chariot destined for the journey of a lifetime. Stonewall had produced signs for the couples that read "Just Married" and "C-BUS of Love." As my mom stepped onto the float, which was surrounded by so many of our friends, I paused to acknowledge how grateful I was for all the support and love around us.

As soon as the float started moving, Josh and I began screaming our heads off to get the crowd engaged. I was yelling, "Please give a round of applause to our newly married couples. These couples were married at the Supreme Court of the United States . . . *for you*!" People cheered. The couples even came up with a little "We are married!" jingle that they chanted.

More than three hundred thousand people cheered us on that day. My dad walked the entire parade route, taking pictures the whole time. My parents were so cute; it was obvious how energized and shocked they were by the huge crowd and the emotion in the air. At the end of the route all the couples exited the float and enjoyed a dance in the middle of a rainbow-clad, smile-filled street. A local musician had written a song, titled "I Do," specifically for the moment. He played it, we all danced, and the tears just flew.

We got up on stage and said a few words to the crowd. One of the couples, Jack and Bill, came up and took the microphone. They said how much we meant to them for everything we had done, and they presented us with a beautiful plaque on behalf of the couples. They also gave us an amazing vacation gift. Josh started bawling as he spoke about the couples and how much they meant to him. I am tough as nails, and very few things can break me down, but watching Josh start crying as he spoke from the heart melted me instantly.

Someone had donated a huge rainbow cake worth more than three thousand dollars. As at most traditional weddings the cake was cut, and the couples fed their spouses pieces of cake in not-so-delicate ways. Josh and I smeared it on each other. This was so special to us because we had none of this when we were married. Ours was a quiet ceremony at the grave of our hero. So now we indulged a little in this wedding reception and relished the memory of our special day. By the time it was over, we were exhausted. Josh agreed to perform again that night at a local bar to thank the owners for all they had done for us. But we couldn't stay out late because we had to address Stonewall and donors at a brunch the next morning.

Over the two weeks leading up to the voyage of the C-BUS of Love, I had army training in Wisconsin, which afforded me some spare time to contemplate what I wanted to say to the brunch crowd. We invited one of the C-BUS couples, Paul and Dennis, to the brunch because we had become very close to them and because they had done so much for the C-BUS project.

Paul is a well-known local painter who also does illustrations for novels. He had created a painting called *Noah's Gay Wedding Cruise*, featuring cameo appearances by couples like Ellen DeGeneres and her wife, Portia de Rossi, and Rosie O'Donnell and her wife, Michelle Rounds, on the deck of the boat. Also on board were Bert and Ernie and various gay animals happily sailing. Drowning in the water were people like Larry Craig, Fred Phelps, Ann Coulter, and many other bigots. Then, before the trip, Paul changed the picture to include Josh and me in his fantasy of heroes for equality. We were so honored; we have that picture hanging in our house to this day.

But more than that, he sold these limited edition prints to help raise money for the C-BUS of Love. It was incredibly successful, so much so that the Westboro Baptist Church and the hateful group NOM (National Organization for Marriage) both weighed in on the controversial subject of the painting. Sales of the painting skyrocketed once these hate groups antiendorsed them. It goes to show that love wins. So we wanted Paul and Dennis at brunch with us.

Karla awarded us with a thick glass award that looked like something out of Hollywood. It had our names etched in it, along with the words "2013 Grand Marshals of Columbus Pride." I knew the speech I had written while on army duty was perfect:

Pride changes lives.

I serve. I serve as a soldier fighting two wars and swearing to protect the Constitution of the United States. I serve as a city employee providing resources to the underprivileged in Columbus. Now I serve as an advocate for the LGBTQ community.

What makes a superhero?

Rosa Parks told people, "At the time I was arrested, I had no idea it would turn into this. It was just a day, like any ordinary day. The only thing that made it significant was masses of people joined in."

Harvey Milk once said, "All men are created equal. No matter how hard they try, they can never erase those words. That is what America is all about." Harvey used those famous words of the Declaration of Independence: "Everyone has the right to life, liberty, and the pursuit of happiness." But what he left out lies just two sentences later: "Whenever any government becomes destructive of these ends, it is the right of the people to alter or to abolish it." Our own Declaration of Independence tells us to stand up for ourselves when people take away our rights.

Leonard Matlovich was the first servicemember to challenge the military's ban of gay people. His fight changed and opened up people's minds. He started the discussion. Coincidentally, the twenty-fifth anniversary of his death was the exact date of this pride march, with "Pride Changes Lives" as the theme.

Each of these superheroes was spot on. Combine all of their messages, and you have people who stood up for themselves and urged people to tell their story. They were arrested, fired, and killed.

Harvey Milk said, "If a bullet should ever enter my brain, let that bullet destroy every closet door."

They all changed many lives and thus, by doing so, the course of history. All of them were living their normal lives and never expected to be a superhero of change.

I married the person I loved at a time when I was home for my R&R in the middle of a war. We could have still been discharged from the army for doing so. We did it from uncertainty of our fate with my deployment after some close calls from mortars. We had no idea what our fate would be. No one does. We honored Leonard Matlovich by exchanging our vows in front of his tombstone that read: "When I was in the military they gave me a medal for killing two men and a discharge for loving one."

When politicians threatened us by saying they would reinstate DADT and kick me out of the military and take away twenty years of retirement for no other reason than loving my husband, while I was currently at war fighting for my country, I challenged that. Josh and I are not legally allowed to be married in our home state of Ohio, so we are fighting that.

When DOMA prohibited Josh from having the right to bury me should I die in war while serving my country, we joined a lawsuit to defeat that law and strike down DOMA. Josh and I were told we had to lie about our reason to change our names. We challenged that. We changed it and set a precedent in Ohio law for all other gay couples in the future.

What does it take to be a superhero?

You don't have to be a soldier to serve your country. You have to tell your stories. If someone passes a law to take away your rights, you have to challenge that. You have to stand up for yourselves and others who are not strong enough to do so. That is serving your country.

I once told the mayor, "It doesn't take an act of Congress to change things; it takes one person at a time."

Pride doesn't change lives; you do. But by having pride in yourself and your community—and coming out and telling your story—you change lives. There is a superhero in each one of us. Any one of us can be like these great leaders before us and change the world.

Thank you very much. This is a great honor, but this is not about us. This is about all of you. So as Harvey Milk famously said, "I recruit you" to be soldiers of change, and if you follow your heart, you will change history.

Following thunderous applause, I introduced Josh. He didn't have any prepared comments but got up and spoke from the heart as he always does. He was emotional, and you could see how much he moved people with his words and his passion. Karla's wife, Linda, came up and kissed us, and she told us we were the greatest grand marshals they had ever had.

Josh had told me several times in the process of organizing the C-BUS of Love that this would be the greatest thing he had ever done. He was right.

21 Activism vs. Politics

Days after the "Pride Changes Lives" parade the decision about DOMA became all the buzz. The Supreme Court kept delaying the announcement right up until the final day it could rule. Everyone was going crazy on the Internet and logging onto the SCOTUS blog. Josh and I had to work that week, but we were just as anxious as everyone else. When I received Josh's text, "DOMA IS DEAD," I couldn't even think. I couldn't process it. Three words meant freedom.

Immediately I thought of Charlie. At her death on February 10, 2013, she was just a little over five months away from seeing justice. That's just 13,651,200 seconds from the eternal peace of knowing her wife and daughter would be taken care of. I kept thinking about how lost I would be without Josh. I think too often we take things for granted, and if anything, Charlie taught me not to do that. This was my reminder that I need to keep fighting so this doesn't happen to anyone else. I sent Charlie's wife, Karen, and her child, Casey, a big Valentine's Day basket full of goodies. My heart was heavy that day and still is. We will miss you Charlie, but we will never forget you. That day's victory was yours.

Shortly after the DOMA ruling Josh and I joined the other SLDN plaintiffs in a conference call regarding a motion by the judge submitted in light of the Supreme Court ruling, requesting response within thirty days on why the court shouldn't rule in our favor. Even better, we learned that SLDN had negotiated that Charlie's death would not prevent Karen's recognition as a spouse entitled to military and veterans benefits. This was a picture-perfect ending to all of this fighting, though even in the midst of such victory Josh and I witnessed the ills of infighting. Politics got the best of OutServe and SLDN, and the groups lost focus at a time when we needed unity the most.

This leads me to the most contentious portion of this book. When I returned from Iraq, there was a major announcement that OutServe and SLDN were joining forces, with one board of directors. I was appalled when I first heard this news, mostly because I viewed SLDN as a much stronger group of professional people with a focused mission. I had placed my reputation and career on the line by letting them represent me. OutServe was a Facebook group, nothing more. It was like Microsoft teaming up with a carryout store on the corner. It made no sense to me, other than the fact that now SLDN could use OutServe's followers as a resource list to communicate with gay women and men in uniform.

The next shocking and unexpected thing was the announcement that Aubrey Sarvis, the director and strategist of SLDN, would retire. He was a very wise man, and when talking to him you always felt like you were in good hands. Allyson Robinson, a transgendered former military member, was appointed as his successor. I had read all about her and thought she seemed to be a good replacement, though my great respect for Aubrey made me instantly judgmental of whoever would try to fill his shoes.

My first interactions with her were not the most positive. I assumed the plaintiffs would be formerly introduced to Allyson, but we never really heard from her. But I imagine she was busy dealing with behind-the-scenes matters, as well as the organization's crumbling finances. When we finally met her, she was charming and eloquent. I thought she did a good job as the voice of the organization. Then, four days before the

DOMA decision was released, Josh yelled out, "Something is seriously wrong." He was reading on Facebook that the board of directors had fired Allyson.

Normally SLDN would have been prepping us for media engagements and lining up interviews for us to talk about how DOMA affects us as servicemembers, but they all quit that day in revolt over the board's decision to fire Allyson. This was one of the most epic fails I had ever seen, and it could not have come at a worse time. There was so much uncertainty for us as people who were involved in a lawsuit against the Department of Defense. Worse, this happened just days after more of the picture came out about the organization's failing finances. I don't know how much of that had to do with OutServe joining SLDN.

As a child I often wondered why acne medication would really cure acne. I figured someone should secretly make it cause acne so people would freak out and have to buy more. A cure means no need for help anymore, so why would the acne medicine company want that? Oh, how the innocent, simple thoughts of a child are actually very poignant. Let's take SLDN for example. To stay relevant as an organization, SLDN needed to have a cause that would prompt passionate people to continue donating money. They fought to end "Don't Ask, Don't Tell" and were successful, but then what? Gay servicemembers were no longer being discharged. Did I think SLDN was still relevant? Absolutely. Transgendered people still cannot serve. Since the fall of DOMA some servicemembers who live in a state with marriage equality will still be forced to PCS (permanent change of station) to a state that doesn't have marriage equality. There are many initiatives SLDN could be spearheading. But now it is gone.

The federal judge presiding over our lawsuit set a deadline of July 18, 2013, which gave the Department of Defense twenty-one days from the ruling on DOMA to issue a stance on our case. On the last day, in typical Republican fashion, the House-controlled BLAG (Bipartisan Legal Advisory Group) waited until the last possible moment to make a statement about whether they would continue defense of these statutes we were challenging.

Keep in mind that this was the same group that chose to waste hundreds of thousands of taxpayer dollars defending a law that the Supreme Court had struck down as mostly unconstitutional. So I wasn't sure how much they wanted to dig in and defend this beyond the DOMA ruling. Our lawsuit specifically challenged uses of terminology referring to the opposite sex in the benefits language for the military, including veterans.

Finally we learned that, in light of the Supreme Court's *Windsor* ruling, they were not going to defend it. We had won! Well, kind of. They didn't want to touch the veterans' portion of the military code for now because none of the plaintiffs in our group had applied for and been denied veterans' rights. This was coming from the Department of Defense, which President Obama had instructed not to defend DOMA. So we wanted to push forward with our challenge. Still, this was a victory for servicemembers, so to me it was almost as important as the DOMA ruling. I have served my country for twenty-four years, and now my country is serving me—which is more than I can say about my state. Our case was still in litigation.

In Ohio same-sex marriage is not legal. The ironic thing, though, is that there are gay people in Ohio who have been able to get divorced. It's one thing to not recognize my marriage. It's another thing to recognize it just long enough to nullify it. The double standard is plain and evil. Everything Josh and I have done is to make this right. There are much larger and more powerful organizations than SLDN, like the Human Rights Campaign (HRC) and Freedom to Marry, that have statewide chapters working on various initiatives for gay people. HRC has done many great things, but this is where I get upset: HRC doesn't think Ohio should take the petition to the ballot to repeal the 2004 constitutional amendment that defines marriage in Ohio as between a man and a woman, at least not just yet.

I know there are smart, strategic people who understand the way politics work and the way funding works in getting people to the polls. I also understand the political games and calculations that go on with looking at who has been appointed and knowing when to strike. What has gone horribly wrong in Ohio is that this opposition between groups who want to legalize gay marriage and groups who want to wait has turned into an all-out war. It's sickening to watch. I have seen gay people almost fight each other because they disagree on a strategy for getting us basic human rights. I understand that there needs to be a strategy, but I watched Charlie Morgan die before she saw justice, without the comfort of knowing that her wife and little girl would be taken care of. This pisses me off, and I don't want to wait another day. Rosa Parks didn't wait, and Martin Luther King Jr. didn't wait. At what point is it okay to say, "This isn't your day to be equal"?

At times we've seen tremendous hypocrisy and what seemed to be completely self-serving motivations. Shortly before the 2012 elections Josh and I were invited to a meeting where we heard representatives from various equality organizations explain how ballot initiatives were too risky, how they have the potential to demotivate the LGBT community and set us back. They pointed to the three states coming up for the 2012 ballet—Maine, Maryland, and Washington—and dismissed their potential for success. Speakers even got up and practically accused the leaders of the petition drive in Ohio of unethical activities during the 2004 elections. We left the meeting that day bewildered.

The most shocking part was what happened just before the

2012 vote. The news started sharing Ohio polls, which pointed to a tipping-point majority preference for marriage equality. Those same equality organizations quickly changed their tune and started posting pictures, sending emails, and selling T-shirts asking for donations to support equality initiatives in Ohio. Seeing a situation like this, you can't help but wonder if a large organization will support equality only if it "owns it." Maybe big groups see grassroots activists as intruders rather than allies, worried that they'll steal donations and support. Can an organization become so large and so dependent on the injustices oppressing its supporters that true equality seems threatening? This is my life: I am not a statistic or a talking point. I am a human being! Don't get me wrong: I'm not saying these big organizations are bad. I just think they have lost their way a bit. Does a cure mean you're not needed anymore? Josh has often said he will gladly put an out-of-business sign on the door of every equality organization when the job is done. I'm not sure everyone feels that way.

Now the rational side of me says that history is changing fast, and there is a tidal wave of support for marriage equality. Many Republicans have even spoken up in support of it, but I don't know if this momentum will last until the next presidential election. And what about all the other Charlie Morgans out there who are dying daily without the ability to protect their families? I guess that's the difference between someone who is an activist and someone who prefers to carefully litigate their way through the system. After serving my country for twenty-four years, I have definitely been molded into what people consider an activist. I want to partake in all these rights and protections I have fought to preserve for everyone else. I can't wait another day for the freedom I was promised in the Declaration of Independence. This book is proof of that.

Josh and I joined the steering committee for the group Freedom to Marry Ohio, led by Ian James, which pushed the envelope by not waiting for other groups and financial backers to support marriage equality. They went grassroots, which is right up our alley, so we signed on. We participated in conference calls, meetings, recruitment of other supporters, and fundraisers (including demonstrating our cooking abilities at a Mongolian BBQ).

Freedom to Marry Ohio established a mandate to place this forty-six-word amendment on the ballot: "Be it resolved by the People of the State of Ohio that Article XV, Section 11 of the Ohio Constitution be adopted and read as follows: In the State of Ohio and its political subdivisions, marriage shall be a union of two consenting adults not nearer of kin than second cousins, and not having a husband or wife living, and no religious institution shall be required to perform or recognize a marriage."

(Section 11 below is what our amendment would replace. The language was later revised.)

"Only a union between one man and one woman may be a marriage valid in or recognized by this state and its political subdivisions. This state and its political subdivisions shall not create or recognize a legal status for relationships of unmarried individuals that intends to approximate the design, qualities, significance or effect of marriage."

DOMA is dead, but states are still permitted to not recognize marriages from other states. Religion has been injected into law, against the vision of our country's founders. So we fight on.

22 Trust the Power of Your Voice

I hope that by telling my story about the life I had to live under "Don't Ask, Don't Tell" I will help people realize what an oppressive and damaging policy this was. I felt so strongly about this that I put my neck on the line to confront those who wanted to reinstate it and forced them to expose their true colors. This is not about sex. This is about hate.

I saw Santorum on the news being asked about the following quote from Colonel E. R. Householder: "The army is not a sociological laboratory. Experimenting with army policy, especially in a time of war, would pose a danger to efficiency, discipline, and morale and would result in ultimate defeat." The newscaster was asking Santorum's opinion after he claimed that the president was playing with "social experimentation" as part of his answer to my question.

Santorum quickly agreed. What he didn't realize was that this was a quote from 1941 addressing racial integration in the military. This exposed hate conclusively for what hate is. There will always be hateful people in the world, but they are the minority. When it gets dangerous is when hateful people become powerful enough to be voted into an influential position, possibly the highest in government. That is terrifying.

The most powerful thing we each have in this world is our voice. We also have our vote; your vote is your voice. A lot of people neglect this power by not utilizing it, but it is important:

it is the only thing we have to protect ourselves from oppression if the wrong people make the laws and rules we all live under.

I was fortunate. I never realized my voice would be heard so loudly. I didn't submit my question to the Republican debate with the intention of it becoming such a big deal. But I really did want to force the presidential candidates not to skirt the issue any longer. I wanted to have each one of those candidates look "gay" in the face and go on record with their prejudices. By "gay" I mean a living, breathing human being with feelings and emotions. I wanted them to look at me while I was honorably serving my country at a time of war, and I wanted them to have the balls to tell me they didn't want me to be there. I figured I would get a politician answer, but I didn't: I got condemnation, even booing. And then I got a manifesto from a bigoted homophobe who was running for the most important job in the United States. I think he exposed not only himself but all of the biased people on that stage.

Josh and I have been fortunate enough to continue having our voices heard—in so many different settings and by so many different types of audiences. We even received an opportunity to be part of the "Story Corps" project and have our story recorded in the Library of Congress . . . the national archives! They wanted military members, particularly gay ones, to talk about their experiences.

We went to Washington and recorded a discussion between us about everything we had done. It is cool to know you're making history, but to know it is literally being recorded and stored for eternity is mind-blowing. Imagine being able to hear a recording of a soldier who fought in the Civil War, describing the things he had experienced. In twenty or thirty years someone will listen to Josh and me and find it hard to believe there was a time when gay people couldn't marry the person they loved. And it will be a struggle for them to understand what we had to go through to make this a reality. But our story keeps all of that heartache alive.

Also in 2013 Josh and I were invited to speak at Middle Tennessee State University. This was a bittersweet invitation because this was the state that had proposed the "Don't Say Gay" bill (SB 49). This was where our activism had started. The house was packed that night. I didn't know it at the time, but there had been contention between the LGBT group that invited us and a Christian group on campus that had agreed to come hear us speak.

I addressed some of the religious arguments against gay marriage, noting that many Christians fight passionately against gay marriage but not against all the atheists and nonpracticing Christians who are granted a civil marriage every single day. I don't see one protest condemning atheist marriage. One would think that if religion was the primary argument against gay marriage, then a Christian would hold an atheist a couple of notches lower than a gay person who believes in God. Not to mention divorce: no one is out protesting that either. If any group has the right to talk about the sanctity of marriage, they need better than a 50 percent divorce rate. So at the end of the day this is not a religious argument. It is just hate. No valid argument that gay marriage will destroy society can be made. Those who deny gay people the right to marry simply don't want them to have the same rights as everyone else. Later the LGBT group on campus told us they had received positive feedback from members of the Christian group who had heard our talk: they were moved by what we had said, and it made them think. I had the same discussion with a soldier from my unit. A divorced man, he told me he didn't believe in marriage equality because of religion. You can imagine how that point of view went over with me. I said, "So you are on your second marriage, and you don't think I have the right to try it once?"

One of our inspirations in the fight against the Tennessee bill was movie star, author, and gay activist George Takei. He has inspired both Josh and me in many ways. First, he decided to come out publicly in 2005. This could have jeopardized his career, but he wanted to be a positive role model. I remember clearly to this day what I thought when I heard about George Takei's decision: I thought how cool it was that famous people were feeling more comfortable about coming out. Some of Josh's early activism was the direct result of George's influence. In particular, when George publicly opposed the "Don't Say Gay" bill in 2011, I was still in Iraq, but Josh, at home, was inspired to activism. He followed in George's "Don't Say Takei" footsteps by creating the "Don't Say H8" website. I recorded a video from Iraq in support of this campaign.

The media also continues to keep our story alive, even when we least expect it. Nearly two years after I was booed for outing myself on national television as a gay soldier, *The Newsroom*, a top-rated HBO show, revisited the event and showed tremendous support. The show's star, Jeff Daniels, plays Will McAvoy, the anchor and managing editor of a show called *News Night*. The third episode of the second season opens with McAvoy at the anchor desk, calling out the GOP presidential candidates for letting the audience boo me during the debate. McAvoy concludes his commentary by saying, "Not one of these 'would-be' commanders in chief took a moment to stand with a line officer. They let him stand alone. Soldiers never do that. Leaders never do that. Witless bullies and hapless punks do it all the time. The only president on the stage last night was Stephen Hill. Godspeed, Captain Hill, and come home safe; a grateful nation is waiting to say thank you."

Incredibly, *The Newsroom* devoted twenty minutes of an hour-long show to my story, though I didn't know this until my phone, my email, and my Facebook page started blowing up as the episode was airing. Now even more Americans know who I am and why I was compelled to put everything on the line to ask that question.

But I want to remind people that this is not about me. This is about thousands of other gay people who have had the same experiences. They are all serving their country to provide our fellow citizens with freedom. They do it under a constant threat, not from an enemy staring at them through the sights of a weapon but from homophobic politicians who wage a war against their civil rights. Fortunately, America saw through this. They responded, and they did it hard—first in their disapproval of what had happened to me on September 22 and again at the polls the following November.

I would like to thank every person who has ever served in the military for their service to our county. I especially want to thank all of my gay brothers and sisters who have served with the additional burden of giving more than just their commitment to their country, giving up their right to be who they are. This is not my story . . . this is *our* story. Live free, brothers and sisters. Be proud of who you are, keep your shoulders back and your head up, and serve with pride.

Epilogue

I have come such a long way, from the days when I could barely accept myself to becoming an activist who stands up for myself and others. I stood up for what I believe in when I asked a question from a war zone, and that simple act showed me the power of my voice. So many times I've gambled and risked everything, but I will never stop fighting for my rights and my beliefs.

I joined a lawsuit with my husband to challenge rules that didn't make sense for legally married same-sex soldiers—one of many lawsuits that challenged the constitutionality of the Defense of Marriage Act (DOMA). When the Supreme Court ruled DOMA unconstitutional, there was still language in the U.S. Code that needed to be changed for LGBT soldiers. Our lawsuit went on for nearly two years, but on October 2, 2013, we received notification that Judge Richard Stearns, of the U.S. District Court for Massachusetts, had entered a judgment in our favor. The court declared that the definitions of "spouse" in Title 10 (Armed Services), Title 32 (National Guard), and Title 38 (Veterans) and of "surviving spouse" in Title 38 are unconstitutional.

I owe a lot to Aubrey Sarvis, David McKean, and John Goodman, as well as the partners at Chadbourne & Parke LLP, especially Abbe Lowell and Christopher Man. I also want to mention all of my fellow plaintiffs who fought alongside of me; I am proud to call them my friends. The plaintiffs included Major Shannon McLaughlin, ARNG, and Casey McLaughlin; Chief

Warrant Officer 2 (CW2) Charlie Morgan (rest in peace, sister), ARNG, and Karen Morgan; Lieutenant Gary Ross, USN, and Dan Ross; Lieutenant Colonel Vicki Hudson, USAR, and Monika Poxon; Airman First Class (A1C) Daniel Henderson, USAF, and Jerret Henderson; Captain Joan Darrah, USN (Retired), and Lynne Kennedy; and Colonel Stewart Bornhoft, USA (Retired), and former lieutenant Stephen McNabb, USN.

But my special callout is to my fallen friend Charlie Morgan. She died fighting for other LGBT soldiers to be free. She will never be forgotten!